Pro Apache Phoenix

An SQL Driver for HBase

First Edition

Shakil Akhtar
Ravi Magham

Apress®

Pro Apache Phoenix: An SQL Driver for HBase

Shakil Akhtar
Bangalore, Karnataka
India

Ravi Magham
Santa Clara, California
USA

ISBN-13 (pbk): 978-1-4842-2369-7   ISBN-13 (electronic): 978-1-4842-2370-3
DOI 10.1007/978-1-4842-2370-3

Library of Congress Control Number: 2016961814

Managing Director: Welmoed Spahr
Lead Editor: Celestin Suresh John
Technical Reviewers: Ankit Singhal and Rajeshbabu Chintaguntla
Editorial Board: Steve Anglin, Pramila Balan, Laura Berendson, Aaron Black, Louise Corrigan,
    Jonathan Gennick, Robert Hutchinson, Celestin Suresh John, Nikhil Karkal, James
    Markham, Susan McDermott, Matthew Moodie, Natalie Pao, Gwenan Spearing
Coordinating Editor: Sanchita Mandal
Copy Editor: Alexander Krider
Compositor: SPi Global
Indexer: SPi Global
Artist: SPi Global

Distributed to the book trade worldwide by Springer Science+Business Media New York, 233 Spring Street, 6th Floor, New York, NY 10013. Phone 1-800-SPRINGER, fax (201) 348-4505, e-mail orders-ny@springer-sbm.com, or visit www.springeronline.com. Apress Media, LLC is a California LLC and the sole member (owner) is Springer Science + Business Media Finance Inc (SSBM Finance Inc). SSBM Finance Inc is a **Delaware** corporation.

For information on translations, please e-mail rights@apress.com, or visit www.apress.com.

Apress and friends of ED books may be purchased in bulk for academic, corporate, or promotional use. eBook versions and licenses are also available for most titles. For more information, reference our Special Bulk Sales–eBook Licensing web page at www.apress.com/bulk-sales.

Any source code or other supplementary materials referenced by the author in this text are available to readers at www.apress.com. For detailed information about how to locate your book's source code, go to www.apress.com/source-code/. Readers can also access source code at SpringerLink in the Supplementary Material section for each chapter.

Printed on acid-free paper

Contents at a Glance

About the Authors.. xiii

About the Technical Reviewers xv

▉Chapter 1: Introduction 1

▉Chapter 2: Using Phoenix 15

▉Chapter 3: CRUD with Phoenix..................................... 37

▉Chapter 4: Querying Data 51

▉Chapter 5: Advanced Querying 63

▉Chapter 6: Transactions.. 79

▉Chapter 7: Advanced Phoenix Concepts 91

▉Chapter 8: Integrating Phoenix with Other Frameworks........... 111

▉Chapter 9: Tools & Tuning... 123

Index.. 137

Contents

About the Authors... xiii

About the Technical Reviewers xv

▓Chapter 1: Introduction 1

  1.1   Big Data Lake and Its Representation 2

  1.2   Modern Applications and Big Data 3

      1.2.1 Fraud Detection in Banking 3

      1.2.2 Log Data Analysis 3

      1.2.3 Recommendation Engines.. 4

  1.3   Analyzing Big Data 4

  1.4   An Overview of Hadoop and MapReduce 5

  1.5   Hadoop Ecosystem... 5

      1.5.1 HDFS.. 6

      1.5.2 MapReduce 7

      1.5.3 HBase 9

      1.5.4 Hive 10

      1.5.5 YARN 11

      1.5.6 Spark... 11

      1.5.7 PIG 11

      1.5.8 ZooKeeper 11

  1.6   Phoenix in the Hadoop Ecosystem 12

  1.7   Phoenix's Place in Big Data Systems 12

1.8   Importance of Traditional SQL-Based Tools and
       the Role of Phoenix 12

    1.8.1   Traditional DBA Problems for Big Data Systems- 13

    1.8.2   Which Tool Should I Use for Big Data? 13

    1.8.3   Massive Data Storage and Challenges 13

    1.8.4   A Traditional Data Warehouse and Querying 13

1.9   Apache Phoenix in Big Data Analytics 14

1.10   Summary 14

■Chapter 2: Using Phoenix 15

2.1   What is Apache Phoenix? 15

2.2   Architecture 16

    2.2.1   Installing Apache Phoenix 17

    2.2.2   Installing Java 17

2.3   Installing HBase 18

2.4   Installing Apache Phoenix 19

2.5   Installing Phoenix on Hortonworks HDP 20

    2.5.1   Downloading Hortonworks Sandbox 21

    2.5.2   Start HBase 27

    2.5.3   Testing Your Phoenix Installation 28

2.6   Installing Phoenix on Cloudera Hadoop 30

2.7   Capabilities 31

2.8   Hadoop Ecosystem and the Role of Phoenix 32

2.9   Brief Description of Phoenix's Key Features 33

    2.9.1   Transactions 33

    2.9.2   User-Defined Functions 33

    2.9.3   Secondary Indexes 34

    2.9.4   Skip Scan 34

    2.9.5   Views 34

2.9.6   Multi-Tenancy 34

2.9.7   Query Server 35

2.10   Summary..35

■Chapter 3: CRUD with Phoenix..37

3.1   Data Types in Phoenix 37

3.1.1   Primitive Data Types 37

3.1.2   Complex Data Types 37

3.2   Data Model 38

3.2.1   Steps in data modeling..39

3.3   Phoenix Write Path 39

3.4   Phoenix Read Path 39

3.5   Basic Commands 39

3.5.1   HELP 40

3.5.2   CREATE 41

3.5.3   UPSERT 41

3.5.4   SELECT 41

3.5.5   ALTER..42

3.5.6   DELETE 42

3.5.7   DESCRIBE 42

3.5.8   LIST..43

3.6   Working with Phoenix API 43

3.6.1   Environment setup 43

3.7   Summary..49

■Chapter 4: Querying Data 51

4.1   Constraints 51

4.1.1   NOT NULL 51

4.2   Creating Tables 52

4.3   Salted Tables 53

4.4   Dropping Tables 55

4.5   ALTER Tables 55

　　4.5.1   Adding Columns.. 56

　　4.5.2   Deleting or Replacing Columns 56

　　4.5.3   Renaming a Column 57

4.6   Clauses.. 57

　　4.6.1   LIMIT 57

　　4.6.2   WHERE 58

　　4.6.3   GROUP BY 58

　　4.6.4   HAVING 59

　　4.6.5   ORDER BY 59

4.7   Logical Operators 60

　　4.7.1   AND 60

　　4.7.2   OR 60

　　4.7.3   IN 60

　　4.7.4   LIKE 61

　　4.7.5   BETWEEN... 61

4.8   Summary.. 61

■Chapter 5: Advanced Querying 63

5.1   Joins... 63

5.2   Inner Join 63

5.3   Outer Join.. 64

　　5.3.1   Left Outer Join... 64

　　5.3.2   Right Outer Join... 65

　　5.3.3   Full Outer Join 66

5.4   Grouped Joins 67

5.5   Hash Join 68

5.6   Sort Merge Join 69

5.7   Join Query Optimizations 69

    5.7.1   Optimizing Through Configuration Properties 70

    5.7.2   Optimizing Query 70

5.8   Subqueries 71

    5.8.1   IN and NOT IN in Subqueries 72

    5.8.2   EXISTS and NOT EXISTS Clauses 72

    5.8.3   ANY, SOME, and ALL Operators with Subqueries 73

    5.8.4   UPSERT Using Subqueries 73

5.9   Views 74

    5.9.1   Creating Views 74

    5.9.2   Dropping Views 75

5.10   Paged Queries 75

    5.10.1   LIMIT and OFFSET 76

    5.10.2   Row Value Constructor 76

5.11   Summary 77

■Chapter 6: Transactions 79

6.1   SQL Transactions 79

6.2   Transaction Properties 79

    6.2.1   Atomicity 80

    6.2.2   Consistency 80

    6.2.3   Isolation 80

    6.2.4   Durability 80

6.3   Transaction Control 80

    6.3.1   COMMIT 80

    6.3.2   ROLLBACK 80

    6.3.3   SAVEPOINT 81

    6.3.4   SET TRANSACTION 81

6.4 Transactions in HBase 81

  6.4.1 Integrating HBase with Transaction Manager 81

  6.4.2 Components of Transaction Manager 82

  6.4.3 Transaction Lifecycle 84

  6.4.4 Concurrency Control 84

  6.4.5 Multiversion Concurrency Control 85

  6.4.6 Optimistic Concurrency Control 85

6.5 Apache Tephra As a Transaction Manager 85

6.6 Phoenix Transactions 86

  6.6.1 Enabling Transactions for Tables 89

  6.6.2 Committing Transactions 89

6.7 Transaction Limitations in Phoenix 90

6.8 Summary 90

■Chapter 7: Advanced Phoenix Concepts 91

7.1 Secondary Indexes 91

  7.1.1 Global Index 92

  7.1.2 Local Index 96

  7.1.3 Covered Index 99

  7.1.4 Functional Indexes 100

  7.1.5 Index Consistency 100

7.2 User Defined Functions 102

  7.2.1 Writing Custom User Defined Functions 102

7.3 Phoenix Query Server 106

  7.3.1 Download 107

  7.3.2 Installation 107

  7.3.3 Setup 107

  7.3.4 Starting PQS 107

  7.3.5 Client 107

7.3.6 Usage 108

7.3.7 Additional PQS Features 109

7.4 Summary.. 109

■Chapter 8: Integrating Phoenix with Other Frameworks............ 111

8.1 Hadoop Ecosystem... 111

8.2 MapReduce Integration 111

8.2.1 Setup 112

8.3 Apache Spark Integration... 115

8.3.1 Setup 116

8.3.2 Reading and Writing Using Dataframe 117

8.4 Apache Hive Integration 118

8.4.1 Setup 118

8.4.2 Table Creation.. 119

8.5 Apache Pig Integration 120

8.5.1 Setup 120

8.5.2 Accessing Data from Phoenix.. 120

8.5.3 Storing Data to Phoenix.. 120

8.6 Apache Flume Integration 121

8.6.1 Setup 121

8.6.2 Configuration 121

8.6.3 Running the Above Setup 122

8.7 Summary.. 122

■Chapter 9: Tools & Tuning.. 123

9.1 Phoenix Tracing Server 123

9.1.1 Trace 123

9.1.2 Span 124

9.1.3 Span Receivers 124

9.1.4 Setup 124

9.2   Phoenix Bulk Loading...127

   9.2.1   Setup 127

   9.2.2   Gotchas...128

9.3   Index Load Async 129

9.4   Pherf...129

   9.4.1   Setup to Run the Test 133

   9.4.2   Gotchas...134

9.5   Summary..135

Index..137

About the Authors

Shakil Akhtar is a TOGAF 9 Certified Enterprise Architect passionate about digital transformation, cloud computing, big data and Internet of Things technologies. He holds many certifications, including Oracle Certified Master Java Enterprise Architect (OCMJEA). He has worked with Cisco, Oracle, CA Technologies, and various other organizations, where he developed and architected large-scale complex enterprise software, creating frameworks and scaling systems to petabyte datasets. He is a longtime fan and an enthusiastic user of open source projects. When not working, he can be found playing guitar and jamming with his friends.

Ravi Magham an engineer passionate about data and data-driven engineering, is experienced in working with and scaling solutions to petabyte datasets. In his past experience, he has worked with CA Technologies, Bazaarvoice, and various other startups. He is actively involved in open source projects and is a member of the Apache Phoenix Project Management Committee (PMC). His current interests are in distributed data stream processing.

About the Technical Reviewers

Ankit Singhal is a software engineer who specializes in designing and developing big data solutions for different lines of business. With over 6 years of big data experience, he has architected and created various analytics products and data warehouse solutions using Hadoop technologies including Hadoop, Kafka, Hive, HBase, and Phoenix. He has a keen interest in contributing to open source projects and has been a committer and a member of Apache Phoenix PMC for more than a year.

Rajeshbabu Chintaguntla committer and a member of the Apache Phoenix PMC, is also a committer for the Apache HBase project. He is an open source enthusiast and has been working on big data projects such as HBase and Phoenix for the past 5 years. He holds a master's degree in computer applications from the University of Hyderabad.

CHAPTER 1

■ ■ ■

Introduction

From the inception of mainframes to modern cloud storage and mobile devices, the amount of data produced has risen steeply. Today, humans produce large amounts of data as they go about their day-to-day activities and business operations. For decades, much of the data produced was not used for analysis or business decision purposes. Nevertheless, data has always been indispensable for both small and large enterprises. Nowadays due to digitalization, the importance and value of data has become an integral part of business decisions. Take the example of online retailers who base business predictions on the basis of user clicks and purchasing patterns—actions that generated a huge amount of data. By applying analytical tools to this data, the retailer gleans valuable information for decision making. One can imagine the flood of data pouring from a smart house or a smart city. These examples give some notion of the huge amount of data and its uses in our public lives. "Big Data" can be seen as comprised of both structured and unstructured data. Figure 1-1 shows some of the big data sources that generate a huge amount of data.

Electronic supplementary material The online version of this chapter (doi:10.1007/978-1-4842-2370-3_1) contains supplementary material, which is available to authorized users.

S. Akhtar and R. Magham, *Pro Apache Phoenix*, DOI 10.1007/978-1-4842-2370-3_1

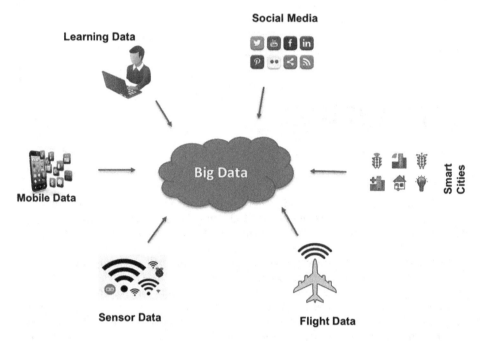

Figure 1-1. *Big Data Sources*

For decades we have been using relational database systems and working with transactional data. In relational database systems, we rarely work with unstructured data as it is deemed less important and only indirectly involved in business activities. When we talk about big data, we mean a mix of transactional data and unstructured data, for example click stream data, sensor data and system logs. Most of us are more comfortable and more skilled in managing transactional data, but more and more often find ourselves handling interactive data that has variety, large volume and high velocity (such as streaming data from a data lake). Unlike transactional data, ever-growing data has velocity characteristics that present significant challenges to the enterprise in both management and analysis. Big data governance can become a tedious task, and lack of expertise and resources can make it difficult for an organization to adapt to this newly-emerging paradigm.

1.1   Big Data Lake and Its Representation

A data lake stores vast amount of data just like water in a natural lake. The data in a data lake usually resides in its native format, including both unstructured and structured data. Requirements and data structure are not defined until the data must be processed.

A data lake uses a flat architecture to store data, unlike the more familiar hierarchical data warehouse that stores data in files or folders. Each data element in a lake has a unique identifier and a set of extended metadata tags. When performing a business analysis involving a data lake query for relevant data, this metadata helps in analyzing the results.

The term data lake is generally used in Hadoop-oriented storage. The data is first loaded into Hadoop cluster nodes, and then data mining and analytics tools are applied to extract business insights from it.

1.2   Modern Applications and Big Data

Today's organizations must manage a vast amount of data from all aspects of their operations. For example, Facebook process more than 500 terabytes of new data daily. A Boeing airliner generates 240 terabytes of data during a single flight across the United States. The data created and consumed by smart phones and sensors embedded into everyday objects generate billions of new data feeds containing information on environment, location, and other information, including video streams.

We can find many such use cases of big data generated from applications, machines, and other means. Let's discuss some of them here. In this section, we will see some big data use cases and their means of generating it.

1.2.1   Fraud Detection in Banking

Increases in digitalization and heavy use of information technology create an increasing number of threats the banking sector. Organizations have to deal with many challenges and must find more innovative and effective approaches to detecting and fighting fraud. Under the traditional model, banks have to work with Business Intelligence (BI) tools and attempt to gain insights by running complex Structured Query Language (SQL) queries on billing and claims data. The problem with this analysis process is the time required—sometimes it takes weeks or months to get results.

With the advent of big data technologies, processing time can be reduced to hours, and in some cases analysis can even be done in real time. There are many tools available to process billions of records and to analyze them by performing intuitive searches via graphical user interfaces. In real time detection, predictive analytics and machine learning techniques have been applied to issue red flag alerts whenever they recognize a pattern that matches a previously known fraud.

1.2.2   Log Data Analysis

Server logs, application logs, and any other informative logs are valuable sources of operational intelligence and finding new business revenue opportunities. We have been using log management and analysis tools since long before big data was in the picture. With the exponential growth in business activities due to e-commerce, Internet of Things, and digitalization, log data has become an arduous task to store, process, and analyze in a cost-effective manner. For example, an advertising agency derives some of its greatest customer insight from analyzing its most transient data by examining its clickstream logs.

Today we can use tools like Hadoop to store and process such big data and draw important information from it.

1.2.3   Recommendation Engines

When you use YouTube, Netflix or other online media services, you may have noticed "recommendation for you" on videos, movies or music. As consumers, we like to have a personalized list for easy access to services and to save time. As we watch more videos, those recommendations become better in accuracy and quality. A more satisfied and happy user is a winning factor for a media company.

Big data makes this easy and cool stuff available to us with its scalability and its power to process huge data either structured (e.g. video titles users search for, music genres they prefer) or unstructured data (e.g. user viewing and listening patterns).

Through big data, data developers can analyze billions of clicks (clickstream data) and process them with the help of machine learning to better provide even more narrowed recommendations for the user.

1.2.3.1   Social Media Analysis

Social Media has emerged as the platform where we discuss most of our daily activities, likes, dislikes, and a lot about personal taste. Companies try to understand a buyer's persona and present recommendations, adjust their pricing, and campaign for optimal results. This data is used to build customer loyalty and find new business opportunities. A big data solution analyzes social media activity data and extracts insightful information from it. There are many big data solutions available for social media analytics such as Google Analytics, Facebook Insights, Twitter Analytics and IBM's Cognos.

1.3   Analyzing Big Data

Big data does not behave the same as traditional transactional data. Big data has many different challenges to manage due to its large data volumes, high velocity of data creation, data type complexity, and extreme time sensitivity. The challenges associated with analytics on big data require a different approach from traditional data analytic processes. For example, content analysis of streaming media requires high-speed processing, storage, and fast analytic techniques. Information gathered from analytical findings can lead to more effective marketing, new revenue opportunities, better customer service, improved operational efficiency, competitive advantages over rival organizations and other business benefits.

Unlike conventional data search, which brings up results based on search strings, unstructured or semi-structured data identifies patterns in text, images, videos, and other such content. Analyzing text is more about searching patterns within documents, emails, and conversations to draw inferences and insights. Unstructured and semi-structured data is analyzed using methods such as Natural Language Processing (NLP), Master Data Management (MDM), data mining, and statistics. These analytics use NoSQL databases such as Hbase and Cassandra to standardize the structure of data that can be queried using query languages such as Phoenix, Hive, Pig, and others.

Business Intelligence (BI) software and data visualization tools are mainly used in data analysis processes, especially in traditional data analysis. But these tools may not fit well with the semi-structured and unstructured data stored in a big data system. Another set of tools including Splunk, Tableau, Pentaho, and Silk, can be easily used for big data analysis and data visualization. Such tools offer their own graphical user interfaces or can be rendered visually with the help of some connectors.

1.4 An Overview of Hadoop and MapReduce

If you are familiar with the Hadoop and MapReduce computing model, you can skip this section. While you do not need intimate knowledge of Hadoop or HBase internals to use Phoenix, understanding their basic principles will help you understand what Phoenix is doing behind the scenes and how you can use Phoenix more effectively with them.

We provide a brief overview of Hadoop and MapReduce here. For more details, you can check Apress books on Hadoop and MapReduce.

1.5 Hadoop Ecosystem

Hadoop has gained familiarity over the years. Below figure 1-2 shows the Hadoop Ecosystem stack. Apache Phoenix works as an SQL skin for HBase that requires basic HBase understanding and, to some extent, an understanding of its native calls behavior. Knowledge about other Hadoop ecosystem components, along with HBase, will be an added advantage in best understanding the big data landscape and in utilizing Phoenix and its best available features. In this chapter we provide an overview of these components and their place in the ecosystem.

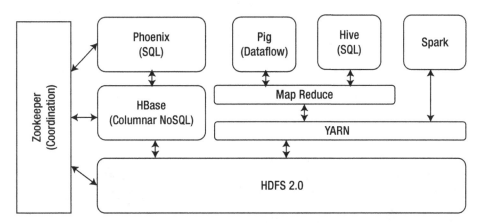

Figure 1-2. Hadoop Ecosystem

1.5.1 HDFS

HDFS (Hadoop Distributed File System) is a distributed file-system that provides high throughput access to data. HDFS stores data in the form of blocks. Each block is 64 MB in size for older versions and 128 MB for newer Hadoop versions. A file larger than a block in size will automatically split into multiple blocks and be stored, replicated on the nodes, by a default replication factor of three to each block; this means each block will be available on three nodes to ensure high availability and fault tolerance. The replication number is configurable and can be changed in the HDFS configuration file.

NameNode: The NameNode is responsible for coordinating and managing other nodes in the system. NameNode acts as the master of the system. It keeps track of files and directories by using a name system with the help of metadata. It manages data blocks stored on the Data Nodes (nodes containing actual data). NameNode can be configured as High Availability with backup nodes in standby and primary as an active node.

DataNodes: DataNodes are machines having actual data (HDFS blocks) in the cluster. In HDFS, the data block size is distributed over a network. Data blocks are replicated on more than one data node to handle node failure scenarios. Data Node servers read and write requests from blocks to the clients.

Secondary NameNode: The secondary NameNode provides backup of data either in memory or local to the disk store. It connects to the primary NameNode periodically and performs checkpoints for backup of metadata in memory. If NameNode fails, you can rebuild the NameNode using this collected checkpoint information. In current Hadoop versions secondary NameNode is almost deprecated and not much in use.

The following figure (see Figure 1-3) shows HDFS components and the data storage of blocks.

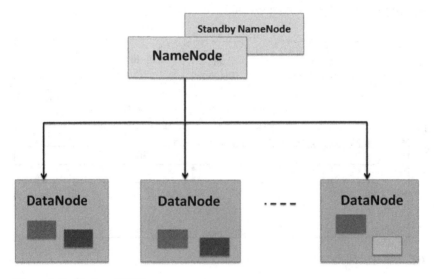

Figure 1-3. Hadoop HDFS

1.5.2   MapReduce

Hadoop MapReduce is a software framework with which we can easily write applications to process large amounts of data in parallel on large clusters of commodity hardware in a reliable, fault-tolerant manner. MapReduce is a programming technique containing two types of algorithm, namely Map and Reduce.

The Map Task: The Map stage or mapper's job is to process input and convert it into smaller parts in the form of key/value pairs.

The Reduce Task: The reduce stage or reducer's job is to process map stage data output into smaller tuples (key/value pairs). This stage combines both shuffle and reduce tasks.

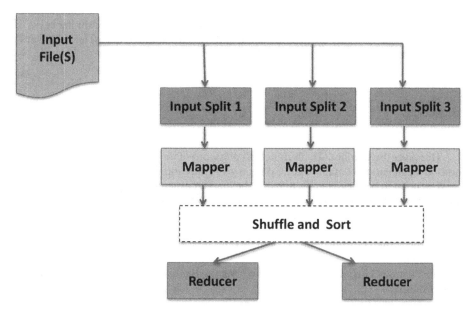

Figure 1-4. *MapReduce*

Let's take a word count example to understand how MapReduce works.

A word count problem is a very basic example, like HelloWorld in Java programming, where Hadoop developers typically start their hands-on MapReduce programming. In the following example, MapReduce is used to count the number of occurrences of each word in the input file.

The word count processing takes place in two stages a mapper phase and a reducer phase. In the mapper phase (done by Mapper), first the input is tokenized into words, then we form a key/value pair with these words where the key is the word itself and value is its count, so here it will be '1.'

For example, consider this sentence as an input to MapReduce processing:

"hello phoenix world by phoenix"

In the map phase, the sentence is split into words, each assigned to an initial key value pair reflecting a single occurrence:

```
<hello,1>
<phoenix,1>
<world,1>
<bye,1>
<phoenix,1>
```

In the reduce phase, the keys are grouped together, and the values for similar keys are added. So, there is only one pair of similar keys, and the values (counts) for these keys would be added so the output key/value pairs would be

```
<bye,1>
<hello,1>
<phoenix,2>
<world,1>
```

This gives the number of occurrence of each word in the input file. Thus, reducer forms an aggregation of mapper keys. We can also apply sorting in the reduce phase.

The point to be noted here is that first the mapper executes completely on the entire data set, splitting the words and making their key value pairs. Only after mapper completes its process does the reducer start. Say we have a total of 50 lines in our input files combined, first the 50 lines are tokenized and key value pairs are formed in parallel (the job performed by each node in parallel); only after this would the reducer start its aggregation.

See Figure 1-5 below to understand how MapReduce processing is done for our word count example.

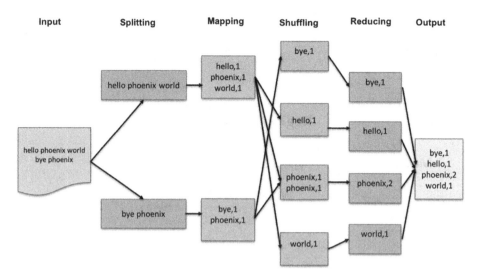

Figure 1-5. *MapReduce processing*

Here we will not describe how to implement MapReduce with Java or any other language. The intention is to illustrate the MapReduce concept.

1.5.3   HBase

HBase is a NoSQL column family database that runs on top of Hadoop HDFS. HBase was developed to handle large storage tables which have billions of rows and millions of columns with fault tolerance capability and horizontal scalability. The HBase concept was inspired by Google's Big Table. Hadoop is mainly meant for batch processing, in which data will be accessed only in a sequential manner, where HBase is used for quick random access of huge data.

HBase is a distributed, column-oriented NoSQL database and uses HDFS for its underlying storage. HDFS, which we already mentioned, works on a write-once and read-many-times (WORM) pattern, but this isn't always the case. Sometimes even a huge dataset requires real time read/write random access; this is where HBase comes into the picture. HBase is built on top of HDFS and distributed on a column-oriented database. Figure 1-6 shows a simple HBase architecture and its components.

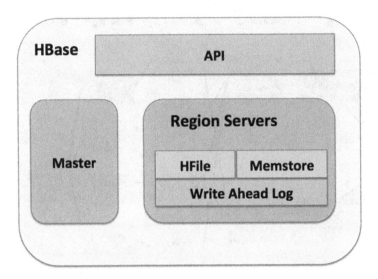

Figure 1-6. *HBase Architecture*

1.5.4   Hive

Hive is an interactive, easy, SQL-like scripting language used to query data stored in HDFS. Although we can use Java to work with HDFS, many data programmers are most comfortable using SQL. Hive was initially created by Facebook for its own infrastructure processing, later they made it open source and donated it to the Apache Software Foundation. The advantage of Hive is that it runs MapReduce jobs behind the scenes, but the programmer does not have to worry about how this is happening. The programmer simply writes HQL (Hive Query Language), and results will be displayed on the console.

Hive is a part of the Hadoop ecosystem and provides an SQL-like interactive interface to Hadoop's underlying HDFS. You can write ad-hoc queries and analyze large datasets Stored in HDFS. Programmers can plug in their custom mappers and reducers when it is inconvenient or inefficient to write this logic in Hive Query Language.

Hive can be divided into the following components:

> *Metastore:* Contains metadata about partitions, columns and the system catalog.

> *Driver:* Provides management for the HQL (Hive Query Language) statement lifecycle.

> *Query Compiler:* Compiles HQL into a directed acyclic graph.

> *Execution Engine:* Executes tasks in the order in which they are produced by the compiler.

> *HiveServer:* Provides a Thrift interface and a JDBC/ODBC server.

Example: A sample hive query HiveSQL

```
SELECT product.product_name, SUM(orders.purchases)
   FROM product JOIN orders
   ON (product.id = orders.product_id)
   WHERE orders.quarter = 'Q1'
   GROUP BY product.product_name; YARN
```

1.5.5 YARN

Apache Hadoop YARN is a cluster management technology and a sub project of Apache Hadoop in Apache Software Foundation (ASF) like other HDFS, Hadoop Common and MapReduce. YARN stands for Yet Another Resource Negotiator. YARN is a general purpose, distributed, application management framework that supersedes the classic MapReduce framework for processing data in Hadoop clusters.

In Hadoop ecosystem, HDFS is storage layer and MapReduce was the data processing layer. However, the MapReduce algorithm is not enough for variety of use-cases. YARN is a central resource manager and distributed application framework that can be used for multiple data processing applications. It reconciles the way applications use resources with node manager agents that monitor the processing operations of individual cluster nodes.

1.5.6 Spark

Apache Apache Spark is an open source fast, in-memory data processing engine, designed for speed, ease of use, and sophisticated analytic. Spark is used to manage big data processing for a variety of data sets ex. text data, graph data etc as well as the source of data (batch/real-time streaming data). Spark enables applications in Hadoop to run in memory that is much faster than running on disk. In addition to Map and Reduce operations, Spark supports streaming data, SQL queries, machine learning and graph data processing. Apart from this, it also reduces the management problem of maintaining separate tools.

1.5.7 PIG

Apache Pig is used for querying data stored in Hadoop clusters. It allows users to write complex MapReduce transformations using high-level SQL -like scripting language called Pig Latin. Pig translates the Pig Latin script into MapReduce tasks by using its Pig Engine component so that it can be executed within YARN for access to a single dataset stored in the HDFS. Programmers need not write complex code in Java for MapReduce tasks rather they can use Pig Latin to perform MapReduce tasks. SQL developers love scripting and Pig Latin comes as their first choice over coding. Apache Pig provides nested data types like tuples, bags, and maps that are missing from MapReduce along with built-in operators like joins, filters, ordering etc.

1.5.8 ZooKeeper

It's difficult to write distributed applications because partial failure may occur between hosts. Apache Zookeeper was developed to mitigate this problem. Zookeeper maintains an open-source server which enables highly reliable distributed coordination.

The Zookeeper framework was created by Yahoo for its internal use and donated to the open source community. Zookeeper is a distributed coordination service that manages large sets of nodes. On any partial failure, clients can connect to any node to receive correct, up-to-date information. HBase is not operational without ZooKeeper. ZooKeeper is a key component for coordination services in Apache Phoenix.

Zookeeper deals with the distributed nature of the application and lets the programmer focus on application logic.

1.6   Phoenix in the Hadoop Ecosystem

Developers who write code may be comfortable with the HBase API to store, retrieve or query data from HBase. Many programmers prefer Structured Query Language (SQL) to writing code in Java or another language. Phoenix is one of the SQL interfaces they can use for querying data from an HBase store. It's a system that gives users the tools to make powerful queries and get results, often in real time. Compared to Hive, Phoenix is highly optimized for Hbase, provides better performance than other similar frameworks, and supports many other interesting features which we will discuss in upcoming chapters. HBase is used as a primary database for Hadoop, also known as Hadoop's database. Phoenix as the SQL interface for Hbase plays a vital role in Hadoop-related big data analysis.

See the following example of a sample Phoenix query that retrieves records from an employee table. If you analyze the query, you will find that it's similar to SQL and easy to write and understand.

Example:

```
SELECT EMP_ID, FNAME,CITY FROM EMPLOYEE;
```

1.7   Phoenix's Place in Big Data Systems

Although Phoenix is not an integral part of the Hadoop ecosystem, it is a necessary tool to work effectively with Hadoop. It is now gaining traction with programmers who write queries to work with HBase data. In this section we will examine challenges in performing big data analysis from a database administrator's perspective and how Phoenix helps to mitigate them.

1.8   Importance of Traditional SQL-Based Tools and the Role of Phoenix

SQL had been the primary tool for interacting with relational database systems for decades. People are comfortable and familiar with this technology and its syntax. In the big data world, there is no standard tool like SQL, but many distributors offer options that provide SQL-like interfaces for querying big data systems. These tools are optimized for underlying support and fast enough to query millions of rows. Phoenix, Hive, and others fall into this category.

If you are a DBA, you may not want to learn or understand Java code to work with data in a Hadoop system. These tools provide that kind of support; you should not have to be a developer to understand the Hadoop API to query data. Phoenix gives you the flexibility to write queries just like SQL when you work with data.

1.8.1   Traditional DBA Problems for Big Data Systems-

A traditional database administrator who has been working on relational databases for a long time is always hesitant about adopting big data culture. What are some of the challenges for a database administrator who adopts big data technology, and what would be the commonly available tools in his or her day-to-day work?

1.8.2   Which Tool Should I Use for Big Data?

You might have used many tools in the past decade to retrieve records from and store data into relational databases. In traditional transactional databases, we might be querying millions of rows. When we talk about big data we are dealing with terabytes, even petabytes of data, or billions of rows. It is quite possible that relational database tools will not work or it will simply take hours, even days, to analyze such a large amount of data. Such slow access might not be relevant for our business purposes if we need instant results to guide some business actions; we want fast results to do business predictions.

Although there is no standard tool available for big data but we have tools that works like relational databases tools support scripting like SQL, such tools are Phoenix, Hive, and Pig. Phoenix can work with petabytes of data and is highly optimized for Hadoop Hbase analysis. This book is about Phoenix; we will see how Phoenix provides these features in analyzing and querying big data storage.

1.8.3   Massive Data Storage and Challenges

Traditional data management and analysis systems are based on the relational database management system (RDBMS). However, RDBMSs apply only to structured data, rather than semi-structured or unstructured data. In addition, RDBMSs are increasingly utilizing more and more expensive hardware. It is apparent that the traditional RDBMSs cannot handle the huge volume and heterogeneity of big data. RDBMS solutions for handling big data are limited by their design and cannot scale on very large data sets. Even to support such solutions requires specialized hardware that increases cost, while big data options like Hadoop run on commodity hardware and are meant for handling such problems in a cost effective manner.

1.8.4   A Traditional Data Warehouse and Querying

In today's organizations, many hundreds of systems may be distributed throughout the company. Each system is largely independent, and any customer experience data is kept within that system. Data warehouses mainly provide storage, more advance querying, and responsiveness to queries more readily than transactional databases without these storage advantages. They can be queried to get useful information from these sources for business decisions in a fast way. Data warehouses are meant to improve the performance of databases.

Generally, we have to face many challenges while getting information out of a data warehouse. These challenges include problems like many incomplete data sources: they do not use the same definitions, and are not always available. For warehouses, data has to be copied to a central location to keep it updated. Copying all data from each of the systems is unfeasible or requires large amounts of time and money. Even sampling the data could be very problematic, as it requires much time and is a costly process. With the help of big data technologies, these problems are mitigated by generating and accessing the data in and from the same big data platform, and we are able to get real time analytics out of it in a fast way for improved business decisions based on these analyses.

1.9 Apache Phoenix in Big Data Analytics

Big data growth is making it essential for businesses to become involved in the use of technologies such as cloud computing and the Internet of Things. Big data analytics are becoming more necessary for organizations to stay on track with market trends. Phoenix and other big data tools are gaining momentum due to their support for comfortable SQL-like interfaces, readability, and rapid learning curves. Behind the wall, Phoenix compiles SQL queries to HBase native calls and runs the scan or plan in parallel for optimization. Phoenix applications can run MapReduce jobs as per user request and utilize big data fundamentals, but the programmer does not need to know about that; he or she should be focusing business logic and writing scripts to access big data storage.

Apache Phoenix is increasing in popularity over other tools available in its space. The beauty is that Phoenix provides features such as skipping full table scan, improves performance of overall system, server/client side parallelizations, filters push down, and Phoenix query server to decouple processing from application, transactions, and secondary indexes. The fact that Phoenix queries are very similar to SQL makes every legacy database admin love it. Certainly, many other tools are available to interact with big data systems for querying and performing analysis, but Phoenix's strong support and optimization for HBase makes it a more likely first choice of SQL interface to work with Hadoop HBase databases. Though it is not a necessary part of the Hadoop ecosystem, it is much in demand for Hbase. Phoenix's integration with big data technologies for ETLs like Spark, Flume, Hive, Pig, and MapReduce makes it a welcome part of the Hadoop ecosystem.

1.10 Summary

In this chapter we discussed big data, some of its uses, and some of the primary sources that generate big data. We also introduced the Hadoop ecosystem as a prerequisite for understanding the role of Apache Phoenix. Phoenix is used as a tool to work with data stored in HBase. Hbase, also known as Hadoop's database, is a column-oriented NoSQL database used primarily for high read-write operations for large tables.

We have been comfortable using traditional RDBMS tools to work with transactional data in a very efficient way. Big data, as such, does not provide those traditional tools, but we have options like Phoenix, Hive, and Impala, which can be used to interact with big data storage and perform operations on it.

In the next chapter we will see how to work with Phoenix, discuss its installation process, and further explore querying HBase data using Phoenix.

CHAPTER 2

■ ■ ■

Using Phoenix

Apache Phoenix is a coating of traditional SQL-like syntactic sugar applied to Hadoop's HBase NoSQL database. It was created as an internal project at Salesforce, later open-sourced on GitHub, and became a top-level Apache project in a very short period of time. HBase, the Hadoop database, is a highly-scalable NoSQL database. You can query HBase data using Phoenix with a syntax similar to SQL as used for relational databases. Apache Phoenix provides a JDBC driver and works as an SQL driver to HBase. Phoenix queries are optimized primarily for HBase and use many Hbase-related techniques, such as skip scan, to improve performance. We will cover skip scan and other advanced Phoenix topics in further chapters.

2.1 What is Apache Phoenix?

The history of Apache Phoenix begins with Salesforce.com, which created Phoenix as an internal project for its need to support a higher level, easy to use, readable SQL language on top of a big data ecosystem. Later, Salesforce.com open-sourced Phoenix on GitHub, and it became a top-level Apache project in May 2014. Now Phoenix is supported by many Hadoop distribution platforms, such as Hortonworks, who provide Phoenix support in their data platform (HDP) versions 2.1 and above Cloudera supports Phoenix in their CDH distribution, and MapR offers easy integration with Phoenix inside their Hadoop distribution platform.

By utilizing HBase as its storage database, Phoenix enables OLTP and analytics for low latency applications in Hadoop by combining standard SQL and JDBC APIs with full ACID transaction capabilities and schema-on-read, late-bound capacities from the world of NoSQL databases (see Figures 2-1). Phoenix supports easy integration with other Hadoop ecosystem products, for example, Hive, Pig, Spark, Flume, and MapReduce.

© Shakil Akhtar and Ravi Magham 2017   15
S. Akhtar and R. Magham, *Pro Apache Phoenix*, DOI 10.1007/978-1-4842-2370-3_2

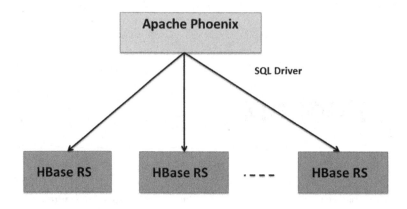

HBase Cluster

Figure 2-1. *Phoenix as an SQL driver for HBase*

Phoenix documentation and releases details can be found at `https://phoenix.apache.org/`. Phoenix source code is hosted on the GitHub repository `https://github.com/apache/phoenix`

2.2 Architecture

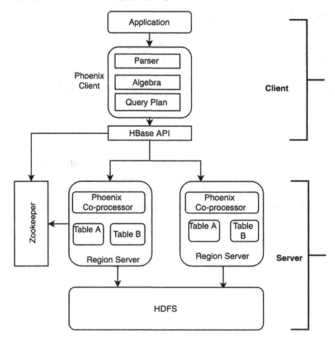

Phoenix Architecture

Figure 2-2. *Phoenix architecture*

Phoenix framework provides the client and server libraries. On the server side, Phoenix custom HBase coprocessors handle indexing, joins, transactions, schema and metadata management. It has custom observers and endpoint coprocessors to support these functionalities.

On the client end, phoenix client library has the parser, necessary relational algebra and query plan components that are used to parse the given query and choose the optimal plan based on cost-based optimization. Once a query plan is chosen, Phoenix internally converts the request to a SCAN, PUT or DELETE operation and executes the operation. The results returned from server are mapped to java ResultSets.

2.2.1   Installing Apache Phoenix

Phoenix requires Java to be installed on the system. In the next section, you will see how to install prerequisite software to get started with Phoenix. Let's start with installing Java then we will see how to install Phoenix.

2.2.2   Installing Java

To install Phoenix, Java must be installed first, along with Hadoop. Ensure you have a recent JDK v1.8.x JVM (Java Virtual Machine) where x is the minor update version. Although only a JRE (Java Runtime Environment) is required to run Phoenix, you will need the full JDK to build the examples in this book that demonstrate how to extend Phoenix with Java code. If you are a non-programmer, the source code distribution for this book contains Phoenix scripts. These can be used to understand Phoenix, work on its features and query data with the Phoenix shell.

You can install Hadoop and Phoenix on Windows, Linux, or MAC OS X systems. We first install Java and set the JAVA_HOME environment variable.

2.2.2.1   Installing Java on Linux

There are many ways you can install Java on Linux. Here we describe how to setup Java in a bash file for all users. You must set up JAVA_HOME environment variable in the /etc/profile.d/ directory. This directory requires root access to change environmental settings. The Oracle JVM installer typically installs Java in /usr/java/jdk-1.8.x, and it creates symlinks from /usr/java/default and /usr/java/latest to the installation.

```
$ /usr/java/latest/bin/java -version
java version "1.8.0_72"
Java(TM) SE Runtime Environment (build 1.8.0_72-b15)
Java HotSpot(TM) 64-Bit Server VM (build 25.72-b19, mixed mode)

$ sudo echo "export JAVA_HOME=/usr/java/latest" > /etc/profile.d/java.sh
$ sudo echo "PATH=$PATH:$JAVA_HOME/bin" >> /etc/profile.d/java.sh
$ ./etc/profile
$ echo $JAVA_HOME
/usr/java/latest
```

2.2.2.2   Installing Java on Mac OS X

Mac OS X systems don't have the /etc/profile.d directory and they are typically single-user systems, so the best practice is to put the environment variable definitions in your $HOME/.bashrc. The Java paths are different, too, and they may be in one of several places.

First you'll need to determine where Java is installed on your Mac and adjust the definitions accordingly. Here is a Java 1.8 example for Mac OS X:

Add the JAVA_HOME environment variable to the location where Java is installed and then export this variable. You can also add these changes in the ~/.bash_profile file.

```
$ export JAVA_HOME=/System/Library/Frameworks/JavaVM.framework/Versions/1.8/Home
$ export PATH=$PATH:$JAVA_HOME/bin
```

2.3   Installing HBase

Before you can work with Phoenix, you must install HBase. Phoenix provides binaries that are compatible with different versions of HBase. Currently Phoenix version 4.7 supports HBase versions 0.98, 1.0, and 1.1, and Phoenix 4.8 release supports HBase 1.2, as well.

To install Hbase, download the HBase binaries and extract the archive from one of the recommended mirror pages:

1.   Select a mirror and navigate to the 1.1.4 directory. If you want to install a different version of HBase, select that version's directory instead, and substitute the version number in place of "1.1.4" in this example.

2.   Inside the directory you will find an hbase-1.1.4-bin.tar.gz file. Download the file to install on your system.

3.   Unarchive the hbase-1.1.4-bin.tar.gz file into some location.

4.   Create the HBASE_HOME environment variable. If you are using a Mac, add the variable to your ~/.bash_profile file:

```
export HBASE_HOME=/Users/hbase-user/Downloads/hbase-1.1.4
```

2.4   Installing Apache Phoenix

Now that we have installed all prerequisite software for Phoenix, the process to install Phoenix is simple. You can build Phoenix from source code or you can use the convenient binary tarfile for a simple setup. It's easy and handy to install Phoenix from the binary distribution. Here we show how to install Phoenix from the binary distribution:

1. Locate the latest Phoenix distribution on the website
    `https://phoenix.apache.org`. The file will have
    a name of the form phoenix-[version]-bin.tar. In this
    example we use phoenix-4.6.0-HBase-1.1-bin.tar.gz, which is
    compatible with HBase version 1.1. If you choose a different
    version, substitute that version number in place of "4.6.0" in
    this example.

2. Download phoenix-4.6.0-HBase-1.1-bin.tar.gz archive and
    extract to your preferred directory.

3. Go to your Phoenix installation directory and copy the
    phoenix-4.6.0-HBase-1.1-server.jar jar to the HBase lib
    directory.

4. We have integrated Phoenix. Now start HBase by executing
    the following script from HBase's bin directory:

    `./start-hbase.sh`

    This will start HBase in standalone mode.

5. With HBase running, start the Phoenix shell by executing the
    Python script from the bin directory:

    `./sqlline.py localhost`

    where localhost is actually the zookeeper quorum address as
    we are running HBase in standalone mode, so the zookeeper
    address is localhost, and 2181 is the default port).

6. Confirm that you see the following as your command-line
    prompt:

    `0:jdbc:phoenix:localhost>`

    This means Phoenix is installed and running.

7. Go to your Hbase installation directory and start HBase by
    executing the `start-hbase.sh` shell script

8. After starting HBase as shown in Figure 2-3, open another
    terminal and start Phoenix (see Figure 2-4)

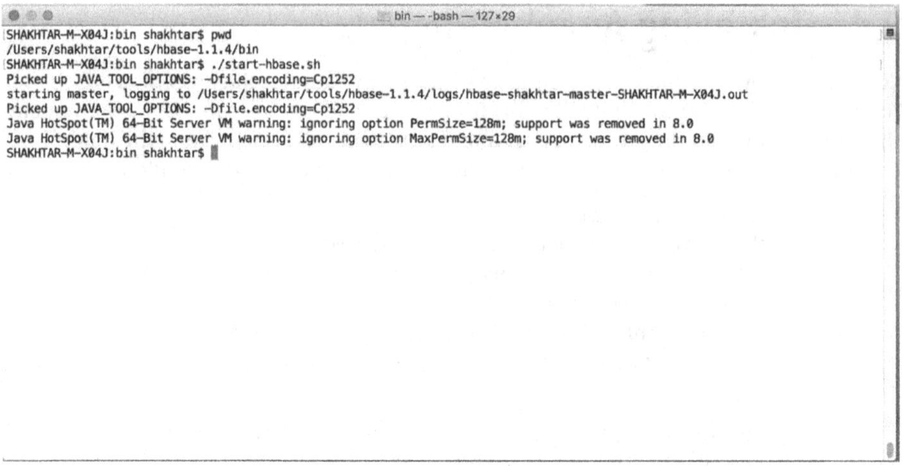
bin — -bash — 127×29
SHAKHTAR-M-X04J:bin shakhtar$ pwd
/Users/shakhtar/tools/hbase-1.1.4/bin
SHAKHTAR-M-X04J:bin shakhtar$ ./start-hbase.sh
Picked up JAVA_TOOL_OPTIONS: -Dfile.encoding=Cp1252
starting master, logging to /Users/shakhtar/tools/hbase-1.1.4/logs/hbase-shakhtar-master-SHAKHTAR-M-X04J.out
Picked up JAVA_TOOL_OPTIONS: -Dfile.encoding=Cp1252
Java HotSpot(TM) 64-Bit Server VM warning: ignoring option PermSize=128m; support was removed in 8.0
Java HotSpot(TM) 64-Bit Server VM warning: ignoring option MaxPermSize=128m; support was removed in 8.0
SHAKHTAR-M-X04J:bin shakhtar$

Figure 2-3. *HBase running*

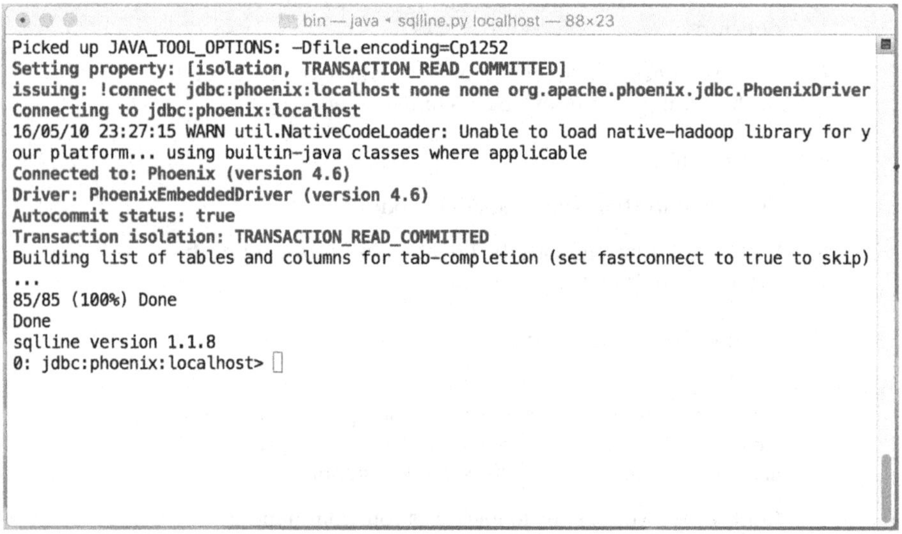
bin — java ◂ sqlline.py localhost — 88×23
Picked up JAVA_TOOL_OPTIONS: -Dfile.encoding=Cp1252
Setting property: [isolation, TRANSACTION_READ_COMMITTED]
issuing: !connect jdbc:phoenix:localhost none none org.apache.phoenix.jdbc.PhoenixDriver
Connecting to jdbc:phoenix:localhost
16/05/10 23:27:15 WARN util.NativeCodeLoader: Unable to load native-hadoop library for y
our platform... using builtin-java classes where applicable
Connected to: Phoenix (version 4.6)
Driver: PhoenixEmbeddedDriver (version 4.6)
Autocommit status: true
Transaction isolation: TRANSACTION_READ_COMMITTED
Building list of tables and columns for tab-completion (set fastconnect to true to skip)
...
85/85 (100%) Done
Done
sqlline version 1.1.8
0: jdbc:phoenix:localhost>

Figure 2-4. *Phoenix shell connected with local HBase*

Congratulations! You have successfully installed Phoenix with HBase.

2.5 Installing Phoenix on Hortonworks HDP

In the bare HBase installation, we saw how to integrate Phoenix with HBase. Now let's install Phoenix on the Hortonworks Data Platform, HDP. HDP is the Hortonworks Hadoop distribution platform. It's easy to install Phoenix on HDP as it comes with HBase pre-installed. Hortonworks provides a sandbox distribution for HDP; we will need to import this as a virtual machine.

Here we use Oracle's open source VirtualBox. You can also install HDP on other virtualization platforms such as kvm or VMware. Check compatibility on the Hortonworks website and download a version of VirtualBox that is compatible to your sandbox. In this example we use the HDP 2.4 distribution. Go to the website `https://www.virtualbox.org/wiki/Downloads` and download VirtualBox for your operating system. In this example, we downloaded VirtualBox 5.0.20 for OS X hosts.

2.5.1 Downloading Hortonworks Sandbox

Download a Hortonworks HDP sandbox distribution from the Hortonworks website `http://hortonworks.com/downloads/`. They have different sandboxes for VMware and VirtualBox. Select the Hortonworks sandbox for VirtualBox. We downloaded the HDP 2.4 sandbox for this demo.

After you have VirtualBox installed in your system and have downloaded HDP for VirtualBox, just double-click on the downloaded file; this will open a VirtualBox window as shown in Figure 2-5.

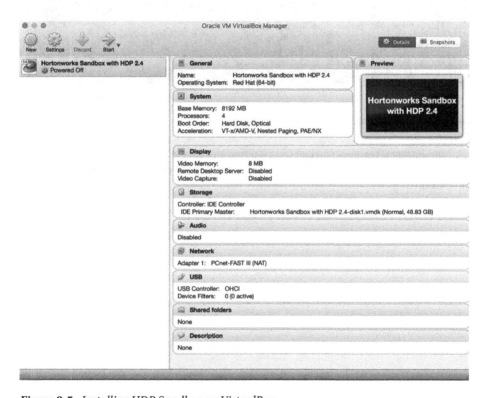

Figure 2-5. *Installing HDP Sandbox on VirtualBox*

Now you configure the vm for the Hortonworks HDP 2.4 platform. (If you are using some other version of HDP make sure you are using a compatible VirtualBox version with it.)

HDP can be started by clicking the power button or just pressing the start arrow.

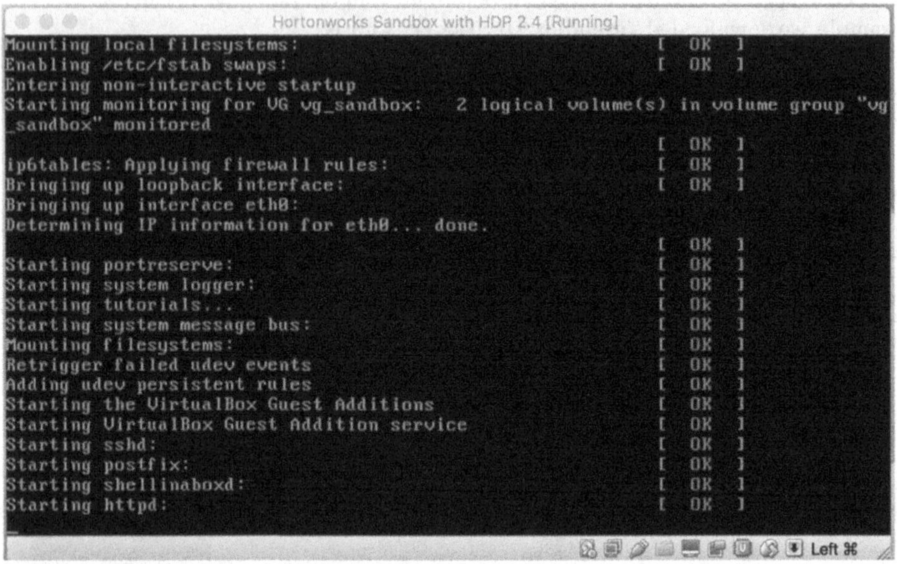

Figure 2-6. HDP Installation running on VM

When HDP is running you will see a window like that shown in Figure 2-7. You can now access HDP. To install Phoenix on top of HDP, we need to log in to HDP and install Phoenix on it.

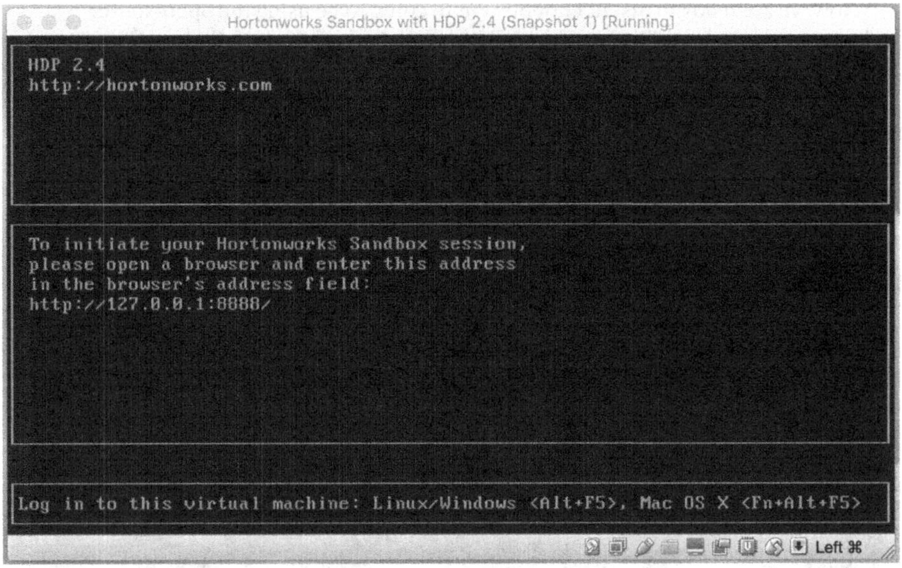

Figure 2-7. HDP installation completed

Log in to HDP with the default username "root" and "Hadoop" as the password. After login, HDP will prompt you to change the password for security. Choose a new password and move ahead.

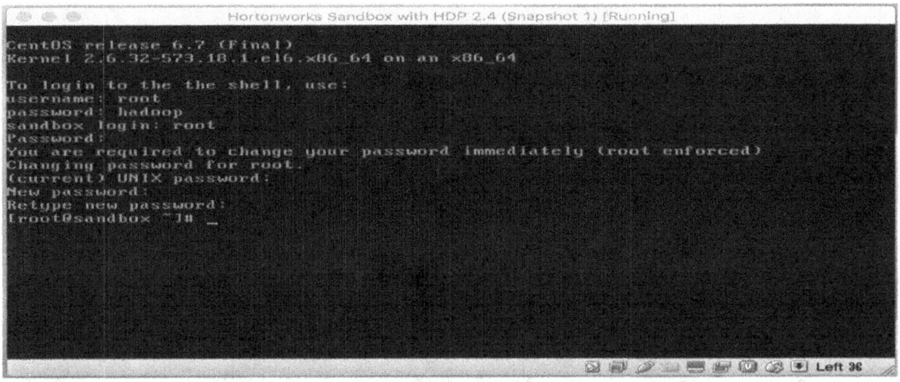

Figure 2-8. Hadoop password creation

Now we are ready to install Phoenix. We're going to be using the open-source package management utility yum to install Phoenix. To start the installation by running the following command:

```
yum install phoenix
```

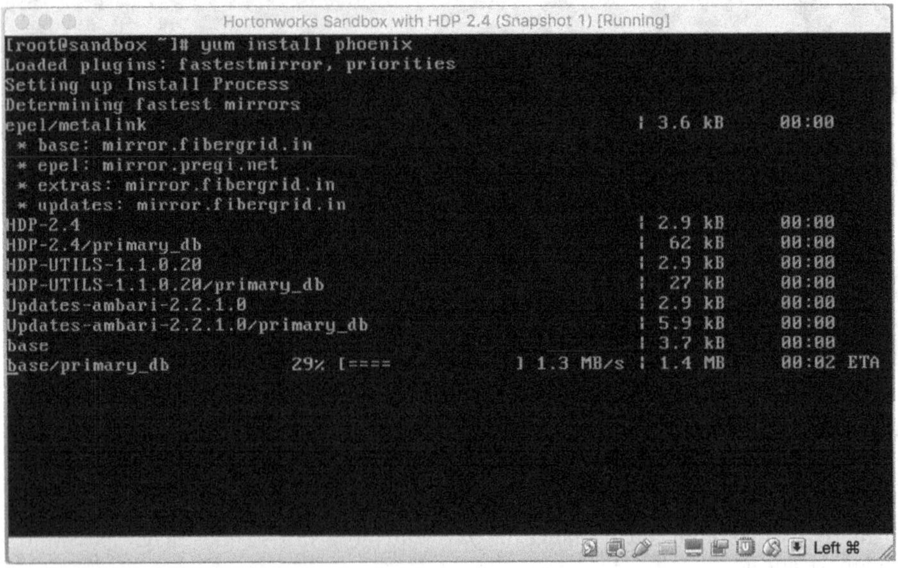

Figure 2-9. *Downloading Phoenix on HDP*

The yum dialog will ask you to download Phoenix. Enter y and proceed. After downloading Phoenix you should see a window similar to that shown in Figure 2-10.

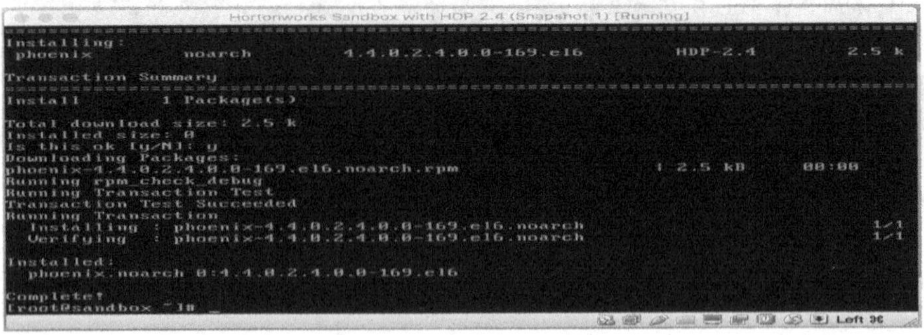

Figure 2-10. *Phoenix download success*

Now that we have downloaded Phoenix, let's configure it to work with HDP.

You can connect to HDP through `ssh` or execute these steps directly on the HDP console.

Once the installation finishes, find your Phoenix core jar file. Locate this file at /usr/hdp/2.4.0.0-169/phoenix/lib/phoenix-core-4.4.0.2.4.0.0-169.jar. Link the Phoenix core jar file to the HBase Master and Region servers.

It's good to connect remotely by ssh. In this example, we `ssh` to HDP running on virtual machine `localhost` on port 2222. Execute the following command from your terminal:

```
ssh root@127.0.0.1 -p 2222
```

Change the version numbers if you have different versions of Hadoop (HDP) or Phoenix.

Figure 2-11. *Check Phoenix prerequisites for executing installation*

```
● ● ●            ⬆ shakhtar — root@sandbox:/usr/hdp/2.4.0.0–169/phoenix/lib — ssh root@127.0.0.1 -p 2222 — 102×36
[root@sandbox phoenix]# cd lib/
[root@sandbox lib]# clear

[root@sandbox lib]# ls
antlr-3.5.jar
calcite-avatica-1.2.0.2.4.0.0-169.jar
calcite-avatica-server-1.2.0.2.4.0.0-169.jar
commons-codec-1.7.jar
commons-configuration-1.6.jar
commons-csv-1.0.jar
commons-io-2.4.jar
commons-lang-2.6.jar
commons-logging-1.2.jar
guava-12.0.1.jar
hadoop-annotations.jar
hadoop-auth.jar
hadoop-common.jar
hadoop-hdfs.jar
hadoop-mapreduce-client-core.jar
hadoop-yarn-api.jar
hadoop-yarn-common.jar
hbase-client.jar
hbase-common.jar
hbase-it.jar
hbase-protocol.jar
hbase-testing-util.jar
jackson-core-asl-1.9.2.jar
jackson-mapper-asl-1.9.2.jar
log4j-1.2.17.jar
netty-3.6.2.Final.jar
phoenix-core-4.4.0.2.4.0.0-169.jar
phoenix-core-4.4.0.2.4.0.0-169-sources.jar
phoenix-core-4.4.0.2.4.0.0-169-tests.jar
phoenix-core-4.4.0.2.4.0.0-169-test-sources.jar
phoenix-flume-4.4.0.2.4.0.0-169.jar
phoenix-pig-4.4.0.2.4.0.0-169.jar
```

Figure 2-12. *Verify that Phoenix core jars are available*

The next step is editing the hbase-site.xml. Go to location /usr/hdp/2.4.0.0-169/etc/hbase/conf.dist and open hbase-site.xml in your favorite editor. Here we use vi to edit the file.

```
vi   /usr/hdp/2.4.0.0-169/etc/hbase/conf.dist/hbase-site.xml
```

Substitute your version numbers in the command line as necessary. In your editor, insert this code between the two configuration tags:

```
<property>
    <name>hbase.defaults.for.version.skip</name>
    <value>true</value>
</property>
<property>
    <name>hbase.regionserver.wal.codec</name>
  <value>org.apache.hadoop.hbase.regionserver.wal.IndexedWALEditCodec</
value>
</property>
```

When you're done, the file should resemble that shown in Figure 2-13:

```
shakhtar — root@sandbox:/usr/hdp/2.4.0.0-169/etc/hbase/conf.dist — ssh root@127.0.0.1 -p 2222 — 89×32
<!--
/**
 *
 * Licensed to the Apache Software Foundation (ASF) under one
 * or more contributor license agreements.  See the NOTICE file
 * distributed with this work for additional information
 * regarding copyright ownership.  The ASF licenses this file
 * to you under the Apache License, Version 2.0 (the
 * "License"); you may not use this file except in compliance
 * with the License.  You may obtain a copy of the License at
 *
 *     http://www.apache.org/licenses/LICENSE-2.0
 *
 * Unless required by applicable law or agreed to in writing, software
 * distributed under the License is distributed on an "AS IS" BASIS,
 * WITHOUT WARRANTIES OR CONDITIONS OF ANY KIND, either express or implied.
 * See the License for the specific language governing permissions and
 * limitations under the License.
 */
-->
<configuration>

<property>
    <name>hbase.defaults.for.version.skip</name>
    <value>true</value>
</property>
<property>
    <name>hbase.regionserver.wal.codec</name>
    <value>org.apache.hadoop.hbase.regionserver.wal.IndexedWALEditCodec</value>
</property>
</configuration>
```

Figure 2-13. *HBase property modification for Phoenix*

Save the file and exit from the editor. These properties will be taken into consideration when your HBase is up and running.

2.5.2   Start HBase

If HBase isn't running yet, you need to start it. Similarly, if HBase is already running, you need to restart it.

Log into Ambari in your browser at 127.0.0.1:8080 with username/password admin/admin. If that doesn't work, check which ip address to use by typing this code in your terminal:

```
ifconfig
```

Once you're logged in, start HBase by clicking HBase on the left panel then Service Actions > Start:

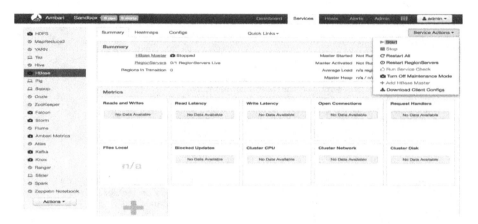

Figure 2-14. HDP HBase service screen

You get a red alert when HBase first starts up; give it a minute or two to start. If the alert persists, you may have to stop another service to free up memory on your sandbox. For example, you may choose to stop MapReduce2 for now. You can always enable it later.

Phoenix should now be installed and ready for use.

2.5.3   Testing Your Phoenix Installation

To test your new Phoenix installation, navigate to Phoenix's bin folder:

```
cd /usr/hdp/2.4.0.0-169/phoenix/bin
```

Run the sqlline.py program:

```
python sqlline.py localhost:2181:/hbase-unsecure
```

This may take a minute or two to start up. If it hangs for too long, check Ambari to make sure HBase is still running.

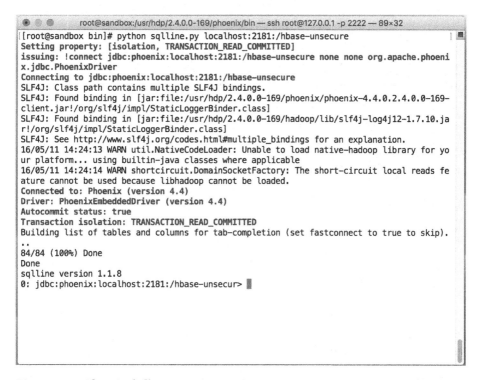

Figure 2-15. *Phoenix shell*

Once the program starts, enter the command !tables, and you will see the window in Fig 2-16:

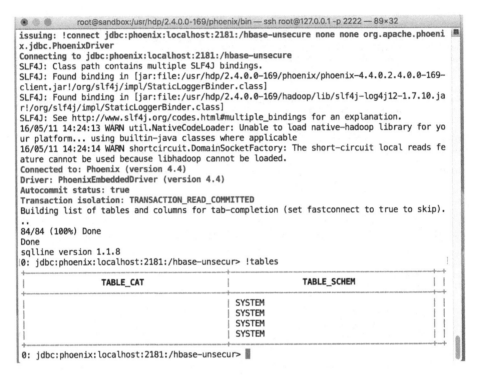

Figure 2-16. *Validating Phoenix successful installation*

2.6 Installing Phoenix on Cloudera Hadoop

Just like the Hortonworks Hadoop distribution, Cloudera has its own Hadoop distribution called CDH. The Phoenix package is currently distributed only as a parcel. Because Cloudera does not support mixing parcels and packages in the same Cloudera Manager instance, you can only install Phoenix into a Cloudera Manager instance that uses parcels. Install Phoenix on Cloudera as described in Cloudera distribution documents.

If you are configuring HBase to use secondary indexes, no WALs can be present in the HBase log directory. To ensure that this is the case, use a fresh HBase installation or perform a full clean shutdown of HBase before configuring Phoenix. We recommend first going without secondary indexes, then when you have a good understanding of the basic concepts you can explore them later.

Install and activate the parcel:

1. In Cloudera Manager, go to Hosts, then Parcels.

2. Select Edit Settings.

3. Click the + sign next to an existing Remote Parcel Repository URL, and add the appropriate URL (`http://archive.cloudera.com/cloudera-labs/phoenix/parcels/1.1/` or `http://archive.cloudera.com/cloudera-labs/phoenix/parcels/1.2/`). Click `Save Changes`.

4. Select `Hosts`, then `Parcels`.

5. In the list of Parcel Names, CLABS_PHOENIX should now be available. Select it and choose `Download`.

6. The first cluster is selected by default. To choose a different cluster for distribution, select it. Find CLABS_PHOENIX in the list, and click `Distribute`.

7. If you do not plan to use secondary indexing, but only plan to use Phoenix for doing simple upsert/select, skip this step. If you do plan to use secondary indexing, add the following to the `hbase-site.xml` advanced configuration snippet. Go to the HBase service, click Configuration, and choose `HBase Service Advanced Configuration Snippet` for `hbase-site.xml`. Paste in the following XML, then save the changes.

```
<property>
 <name>hbase.regionserver.wal.codec</name>

 <value>org.apache.hadoop.hbase.regionserver.wal.IndexedWALEditCodec</value>
</property>

To configure the IndexedWALEditCodec, see https://phoenix.apache.org/
secondary_indexing.html.
Click Actions > Restart.
```

From a shell, execute `phoenix-sqlline.py localhost:2181`. If you have a different port configured for Phoenix, use that port in the command. This will open the Phoenix shell.

Now you are ready to write some SQL. To see available tables, execute the SQL command **!tables** on the Phoenix console.

2.7 Capabilities

Phoenix is an open source SQL driver for HBase. It converts standard JDBC APIs to native HBase calls to create tables, insert data, and query HBase data. In this section we provide an introductory description of Phoenix features. We will discuss them in detail in later chapters.

- Common SQL data types
- Inserts and updates

- SELECT, DISTINCT, GROUP BY, HAVING

- NOT NULL and primary key constraints

- Inner and outer JOINs

- Views

- Subqueries

- Improving query performance on non-row key columns with Secondary Indexes

- Spark integration

- User Defined Functions to allow users to create and deploy their own custom or domain-specific functions to the cluster

- Transactions

- Statistics collection

- Dynamic columns

- Query server

- Multi-tenancy

2.8   Hadoop Ecosystem and the Role of Phoenix

Hadoop has become established as a primary source for big data analytics. It has various components and technologies in its ecosystem. HBase, a non-relational distributed database, is one of the components used for column data model storage. Hbase, known as Hadoop database, supports random, real-time read and write operations in very large column-oriented tables. It is used as the backing system for MapReduce jobs.

We can use the HBase API for database operations on HBase. Phoenix is a high performance SQL skin for HBase used to provide the user an interactive SQL interface for writing efficient, high performance queries. Figure 2-17 illustrates high-level Phoenix working with a Hadoop HBase database.

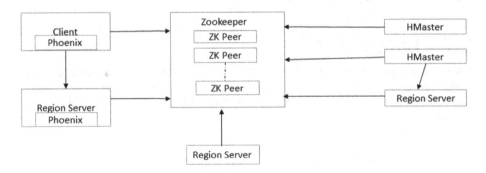

Figure 2-17. Phoenix communicating with HBase

There are SQL interfaces for Hadoop other than Phoenix, such as Apache Hive and Cloudera Impala. Table 2-1 presents a comparison of these three and their features. Hive is a powerful querying engine for the Hadoop ecosystem, but Phoenix is Hbase-specific and highly optimized for it. Phoenix advantages that give it better performance than other alternatives include support for secondary indexes, transactions, and user defined functions.

Table 2-1. *Comparison of Phoenix, Hive, and Impala*

	Phoenix	Hive	Impala
Syntax	SQL	Hive QL	SQL
Key Goal	High performance SQL queries over HBase for low- latency applications	Batch processing	Interactive exploratory analytics on large data sets
Secondary Indexes	Yes(Non ACID compliant)	No	No
Dedicated Daemons	Yes	Yes	Yes
HBase Specific?	Yes	No	No

2.9 Brief Description of Phoenix's Key Features

Let's discuss some of the key features of Phoenix we will be using while taking a deep dive in our examples. This is just an overview; in later chapters we will discuss them in detail.

2.9.1 Transactions

Phoenix provides transaction support with full ACID semantics with the help of Apache Tephra for HBase row-level transactional semantics. Apache Tephra provides snapshot isolation of concurrent transactions by implementing multi-versioned concurrency control. At the time of this writing, Tephra is an Apache incubator project.

2.9.2 User-Defined Functions

You can create temporary or permanent user-defined or domain-specific scalar functions. User defined functions can be used in the same way as built-in functions in queries such as SELECT, DELETE, and UPSERT to create functional indexes. Temporary functions are specific to a connection and are not accessible in other connections. For permanent functions, meta-information is stored in a system table called SYSTEM.FUNCTION. Phoenix supports tenant-specific functions. Functions created in a tenant-specific session or connection are not visible to other tenant-specific sessions or connections. Only global tenant (a.k.a. no tenant) specific functions are visible to all the connections.

2.9.3   Secondary Indexes

Secondary indexes are not like primary indexes, and may have duplicate values. For example, a customer name can have similar values. Generally, primary keys are created in the database when the table is activated. Secondary indexes are created for a large frequently accessed table when primary index sorting is not possible or hard to apply. HBase does not have indexes. The row key is sorted in sort order and the access pattern is based on row key. Orthogonal access patterns require a full scan of the table. Secondary indexes created on alternate row keys can allow point lookup (accessed using get() operations), are much faster, and do not require a full scan on the table.

2.9.4   Skip Scan

Skip scan uses column(s) of a composite index to find distinct values. The first matched value is skipped along with the index until it finds the next value. Skip scan significantly improves query performance over a range and on full scans on a given set of keys while retrieving rows.

The skip scan utilizes the SEEK_NEXT_USING_HINT enum of the HBase filter. It specifies the next key to seek given as a hint by the filter. It stores details about what set of keys are being searched for in each column. It then takes a key, and figures out whether it is one of the combinations. If not, it evaluates the next highest key to which to jump.

2.9.5   Views

Phoenix supports view syntax as in standard SQL to enable multiple virtual tables to all share the same underlying physical HBase table. There are many limitations for views in Phoenix; you can find them in the Phoenix reference documentation at `https://phoenix.apache.org/views.html`. This feature is very important in HBase, as you cannot realistically keep more than a hundred physical tables and continue getting reasonable performance from HBase.

2.9.6   Multi-Tenancy

Phoenix offers multi-tenancy by declaring it while creating tables with tenant-specific configuration properties. The tenant-specific connection has to be injected by supplying a tenant id at the time of connection. Once the connection is opened you can access that tenant data. Tenants can see all data in regular tables, but see only their own data in multi-tenant tables.

You can create tenant-specific views on top of multi-tenant-tables and add your own columns to the views.

2.9.7   Query Server

Phoenix Query Server is a way to support other Java clients. It has an inbuilt stand-alone server that exposes a thin client. The thin client uses JSON to interact with the Phoenix query server (PQS). The query server is an HTTP server that supports two transport mechanisms, JSON and Protocol Buffers, for communications to the clients. Protocol buffers are the default in PQS and more efficient than JSON. The thin client is built using Apache Calcite's Avatica component.

You can write your clients in C#, Python, or other languages by utilizing this beautiful feature. You will see more on query server in later sections of this book.

2.10   Summary

Apache Phoenix is an open source SQL driver for Hadoop's HBase database. It is used to query HBase data by writing simple SQL-like queries. Phoenix can be installed with HBase running in standalone or distributed environments. It is available with the Hortonworks Data Platform or the Cloudera Hadoop distribution.

In the upcoming chapters, we will discuss Phoenix syntax and CRUD operations for HBase data and query optimization techniques.

CHAPTER 3

■ ■ ■

CRUD with Phoenix

Now that we have installed Phoenix and HBase, let's get started with performing the basic operations of CREATE, UPDATE, DELETE and SELECT using SQL. Let's also take a dive into the data types and perform CRUD operations from the "Sqlline" CLI available in Phoenix.

3.1 Data Types in Phoenix

Unlike HBase which is data-type agnostic, Phoenix provides a set of data types that specify the type of data that the column holds. Each data type is internally mapped to a corresponding data type of either Java or SQL. There are Unsigned versions of the numeric and time data types that hold only positive values. The Unsigned versions of the time data types are needed when the value has been serialized by the HBase utility method `org.apache.hadoop.hbase.utils.Bytes`.

3.1.1 Primitive Data Types

Phoenix framework provides a custom DataType mapping to various types defined in java.sql.Types unlike in HBase where all the data is just stored as bytes in big endian notation. Each datatype has a codec to decode the raw bytes to java primitives. The supported data types are boolean, char, varchar, decimal, int, short, long, float, double, date and time . For each of the numerical data types there is an associated unsigned version to handle positive values.

3.1.2 Complex Data Types

HBase gives you freedom in what and how you store, and Phoenix gives you its methods. Similar to other platforms support of the complex types like STRUCT, ARRAY , Phoenix only supports Array type.

See Table 3-1 for frequently used available data types in Phoenix and their corresponding Java mappings.

© Shakil Akhtar and Ravi Magham 2017
S. Akhtar and R. Magham, *Pro Apache Phoenix*, DOI 10.1007/978-1-4842-2370-3_3

Table 3-1. *Phoenix data types*

Data Type	Java Mapping	Notes
TINYINT	java.lang.Byte	
SMALLINT	java.lang.Short	
INTEGER	java.lang.Integer	
BIGINT	java.lang.BigInteger	
FLOAT	java.lang.Float	
DOUBLE	java.lang.Double	
DECIMAL	java.math.BigDecimal	Can specify fixed precision and scale.
BOOLEAN	java.lang.Boolean	True/False. Mapped internally to 0/1.
TIME	java.sql.Time. The default format is yyyy-MM-ddhh:mm:ss	Internal representation based on number of milliseconds since the epoch in GMT
VARCHAR	java.lang.String	Variable length string mapped internally in UTF8
CHAR	java.lang.String	Fixed length string mapped internally in UTF8
BINARY	byte[]	Fixed length byte array.
VARBINARY	byte[]	Variable length byte array.
ARRAY	java.sql.Array.	Every primitive type except VARBINARY may be declared as a single dimension ARRAY.

3.2   Data Model

Apart from many similarities of Phoenix with relation databases like organizing data as rows and columns into tables, there are couple of significant differences. Each table in Phoenix must contain atleast one column family. Simply put, a column family allows us to group a set of columns into one to which we can specify separates tuning and storage specifications at table creation time. Each column is versioned and the column content is an uninterrupted byte array. Each row is uniquely identified by a row key. Data is apparently stored physically on a per column family basis as separate HFiles on disk.

3.2.1   Steps in data modeling

As in designing relational systems, the steps in designing the data model in Phoenix involves

1. Analyzing requirements

2. Identifying entities and their relationships

3. Identify queries

4. Define the schema

In a relational system, the focus and effort is more around describing entities and its interactions and less about the kind of queries that will be run . However, in Phoenix more focus should be given in identifying the query access patterns and then come up with a schema aligned to meet it.

Additionally we should avoid trying to create normalized tables as joins are a costly call.

3.3   Phoenix Write Path

When an UPSERT statement is issued, Phoenix parses the query and converts to a HBase Put operation. This operation does the functionality of an INSERT of a new row or UPDATE of an existing row. A write by default when received by a Region server is first written off to it Write Ahead Log(WAL) and Memstore. Writes to WAL ensure durability. A write is considered complete only when the change is written to the two places.

3.4   Phoenix Read Path

A SELECT query allows for reading data from multiple tables. Once the query is parsed by Phoenix, it prepares a set of query plans and chooses an optimal one based on various criterias like indexes on table. The optimal plan is then materialized into a set of HBase Scan operations which are executed in parallel using an ExecutorService pool. The results are merged on the client.

3.5   Basic Commands

In this section, we do not elaborate on the detailed working of Phoenix commands, instead we just touch upon things to get some hands-on experience. We will add more sugar to these concepts in the next chapter where we explain more advanced Phoenix concepts.

Let's get started by running basic SQL commands, as if you were merely using a SQL database, from the CLI **sqlline.py**. To run sqlline.py, create a new terminal window, navigate to the binary distribution directory(bin) on the machine and type the following command.

```
$ python sqlline.py localhost:2181:/hbase

Setting property: [isolation, TRANSACTION_READ_COMMITTED]
issuing: !connect jdbc:phoenix:localhost:2181:/hbase none none
org.apache.phoenix.jdbc.PhoenixDriver
Connecting to jdbc:phoenix:localhost:2181:/hbase

.....

.....
Connected to: Phoenix (version 4.4)
Driver: PhoenixEmbeddedDriver (version 4.4)
Autocommit status: true
Transaction isolation: TRANSACTION_READ_COMMITTED
Building list of tables and columns for tab-completion (set fastconnect to true to skip)...
84/84 (100%) Done
Done
sqlline version 1.1.8
0: jdbc:phoenix:localhost:2181:/hbase>
```

■ **Note** By default, Phoenix upper-cases all column names and table names defined in the table. If you are Looking case-sensitive, enclose each column name with "double quotes."

3.5.1 HELP

To request help from the shell, type **!help** to see the list of available commands.

■ **Note** These commands correspond to Phoenix Sqlline. For other JDBC clients you can refer to their manuals.

```
jdbc:phoenix:localhost:2181:/hbase> !help
```

3.5.2   CREATE

Let's create a simple *user* table with 'id' as a primary key. Note that the columns *first_name* and *last_name* are mapped to the 'd' column family. If no column family is specified, the column is internally mapped to the '*0*' column family. You can override the default column family by defining the DDL property DEFAULT_COLUMN_FAMILY=column_family_name while creating tables.

```
jdbc:phoenix:localhost:2181:/hbase>·CREATE·TABLE·user(id·INTEGER·
NOT·NULL·PRIMARY·KEY·, ·d.first_name·VARCHAR·, ·d.last_name·
VARCHAR);¤
```

3.5.3   UPSERT

Let's upsert two rows. Care should be taken to ensure the integrity constraints defined are honored. Here, we explicitly set the value for the id column. Phoenix does provide a 'SEQUENCE' feature for providing a monotonically increasing value to a column.

Internally, the SQL call is converted into an HBase Put mutation.

```
0: jdbc:phoenix:localhost:2181:/hbase> UPSERT INTO USER VALUES (1, 'shakil',
'soz');

0: jdbc:phoenix:localhost:2181:/hbase> UPSERT INTO USER VALUES (2, 'ravi',
'magham');
```

3.5.4   SELECT

SELECT retrieves data from one or more tables, and can include a UNION ALL to combine rows from multiple SELECT statements.

```
0: jdbc:phoenix:localhost:2181:/hbase> SELECT FIRST_NAME FROM USER;
```

Do a quick start of your HBase Shell and perform a *scan 'USER'*; you should see two rows with each row having three columns. You may be surprised to see column *D:_0*. In the next chapter we will discuss the purpose of '0'.

3.5.5 ALTER

The ALTER command allows us to alter the schema of a table. You can add or drop columns, and can update the table options. Let's try adding a zipcode column to the user table.

```
0: jdbc:phoenix:localhost:2181/hbase-unsecure> ALTER TABLE USER ADD zipcode INTEGER;
No rows affected (6.037 seconds)
0: jdbc:phoenix:localhost:2181/hbase-unsecure> !describe user;
```

TABLE_CAT	TABLE_SCHEM	TABLE_NAME	COLUMN_NAME	DATA_TYPE
		USER	ID	4
		USER	FIRST_NAME	12
		USER	LAST_NAME	12
		USER	ZIPCODE	4

```
0: jdbc:phoenix:localhost:2181/hbase-unsecure> ▌
```

3.5.6 DELETE

The DELETE statement deletes the rows matching the WHERE clause from the underlying table.

```
0: jdbc:phoenix:localhost:2181:/hbase> delete from user where id = 1;
```

```
0: jdbc:phoenix:localhost:2181/hbase-unsecure> delete from user where id = 1;
1 row affected (0.014 seconds)
0: jdbc:phoenix:localhost:2181/hbase-unsecure> ▌
```

3.5.7 DESCRIBE

DESCRIBE is an Sqlline command. The statement allows us to view the schema defined for a table. All metadata about the tables and the schema of the column names and the data types is stored in a table named SYSTEM.CATALOG. The following query fetches the schema from the CATALOG table.

```
0: jdbc:phoenix:localhost:2181:/hbase> !describe user
```

3.5.8   LIST

To get a list of the set of tables in the database, execute the following Sqlline command. List is also an Sqlline command, as is DESCRIBE, as we mentioned above.

```
0: jdbc:phoenix:localhost:2181:/hbase> !list
```

```
0: jdbc:phoenix:localhost:2181/hbase-unsecure> !tables
```

TABLE_CAT	TABLE_SCHEM	TABLE_NAME	TABLE_TYPE	REMARKS
	SYSTEM	CATALOG	SYSTEM TABLE	
	SYSTEM	FUNCTION	SYSTEM TABLE	
	SYSTEM	SEQUENCE	SYSTEM TABLE	
	SYSTEM	STATS	SYSTEM TABLE	
		USER	TABLE	

```
0: jdbc:phoenix:localhost:2181/hbase-unsecure>
```

3.6   Working with Phoenix API

Now you understand Phoenix CLI and how to work with it. Phoenix Command Line Interface is an intuitive and easy to use interface to work with big data analysis and has been popular tool among SQL developers. Phoenix also provides APIs for developers who write code. APIs are written in Java and easy to use. Developers can use them similar like other Java libraries in their projects.

In the following section, you will see how to work with Phoenix API using popular eclipse IDE and maven as a build mechanism.

3.6.1   Environment setup

To work with Phoenix API, you need an editor or IDE for faster development. Eclipse, an open source IDE has been most popular Java IDE since decade. We are using eclipse mars in our example. You can download eclipse from `https://eclipse.org/downloads/` Make sure you have Java installed to work with eclipse. Create a maven project in eclipse in our example we create project pro-apache-phoenix. Maven is used for build, packaging and dependency management for your project. See Figure 3-1 setting maven project.

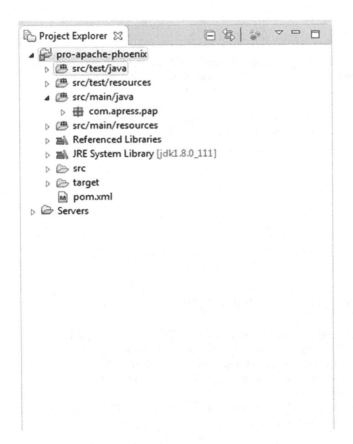

Figure 3-1. *Setting up maven project*

You must add phoenix maven dependencies along with HBase dependencies. We need HBase dependencies as Phoenix works with HBase. Choose your phoenix and HBase compatible versions. You can find Phoenix versions compatibility for HBase on Phoenix website. Now we have created maven project let's see what's inside maven dependencies. Your maven pom file should look like below if you are using same version as in this example.

```
<project xmlns="http://maven.apache.org/POM/4.0.0" xmlns:xsi="http://www.
w3.org/2001/XMLSchema-instance"
xsi:schemaLocation="http://maven.apache.org/POM/4.0.0 http://maven.apache.
org/xsd/maven-4.0.0.xsd">
<modelVersion>4.0.0</modelVersion>
  <groupId>com.apress.phoenix</groupId>
  <artifactId>pro-apache-phoenix</artifactId>
  <version>0.0.1-SNAPSHOT</version>
  <name>pro-apache-phoenix</name>
```

```xml
    <description>Pro Apache Phoenix Source Code </description>

    <properties>
        <java.version>1.8</java.version>
        <phoenix.version>4.8.0-HBase-1.1</phoenix.version>
        <junit.version>4.11</junit.version>
        <project.build.sourceEncoding>UTF-8</project.build.sourceEncoding>
    </properties>

<dependencies>
    <dependency>
        <groupId>org.apache.phoenix</groupId>
        <artifactId>phoenix-core</artifactId>
        <version>${phoenix.version}</version>
    </dependency>
    <dependency>
        <groupId>junit</groupId>
        <artifactId>junit</artifactId>
        <version>${junit.version}</version>
        <scope>test</scope>
    </dependency>
</dependencies>

<build>
<plugins>
<plugin>
<groupId>org.apache.maven.plugins</groupId>
<artifactId>maven-compiler-plugin</artifactId>
<configuration>
<source>${java.version}</source>
<target>${java.version}</target>
<encoding>${project.build.sourceEncoding}</encoding>
<debug>true</debug>
</configuration>
</plugin>
            <plugin>
                <groupId>org.apache.maven.plugins</groupId>
                <artifactId>maven-jar-plugin</artifactId>
                <configuration>
                    <archive>
                        <manifest>
                            <addClasspath>true</addClasspath>
                            <classpathPrefix>lib/</classpathPrefix>
                            <mainClass>com.apress.pap.PhoenixJdbc</
                            mainClass>
                        </manifest>
                    </archive>
                </configuration>
```

```
            </plugin>
            <plugin>
                <groupId>org.apache.maven.plugins</groupId>
                <artifactId>maven-dependency-plugin</artifactId>
                <executions>
                    <execution>
                        <id>copy</id>
                        <phase>install</phase>
                        <goals>
                            <goal>copy-dependencies</goal>
                        </goals>
                        <configuration>
                            <outputDirectory>${project.build.directory}/
                            lib</outputDirectory>
                        </configuration>
                    </execution>
                </executions>
            </plugin>
        </plugins>
    </build>
</project>
```

The first dependency entry in the POM file imports the Phoenix Core Maven dependency, which provides access to the Phoenix JDBC drive. It sets the source compilation to Java 8, specifies that dependencies should be copied to the target/lib folder during the build, and makes the resulting JAR file executable for the main class, com.apress.pap.PhoenixJdbc. After adding all dependencies to maven pom.xml run mvn clean install that will install all required libraries into your local maven repository and add them to your project compilation unit. Once done, you can start using Phoenix API. In our project, we created one java class PhoneixJdbc.java . Let's explore PhoenixJdbc source code.

```java
package com.apress.pap;

import java.sql.Connection;
import java.sql.DriverManager;
import java.sql.PreparedStatement;
import java.sql.ResultSet;
import java.sql.SQLException;
import java.sql.Statement;

/**
 * Using Phoenix API for CRUD Operations
 */
public class PhoenixJdbc {

        public static void main(String[] args) {
                Connection connection = null;
```

```java
Statement statement = null;
ResultSet rs = null;
PreparedStatement ps = null;

try {

        Class.forName("org.apache.phoenix.jdbc.
        PhoenixDriver");
        // Connect to the database
        connection = DriverManager.getConnection("jdbc:phoen
        ix:localhost:2181:/hbase");
        System.out.println("Connection established....");
        // Create a JDBC statement
        statement = connection.createStatement();

        // Execute our statements
        statement.executeUpdate(
                    "create table user (id INTEGER NOT
                    NULL PRIMARY KEY, d.first_name
                    VARCHAR,d.last_name VARCHAR)");
        statement.executeUpdate("upsert into user values
        (1,'John','Mayer')");
        statement.executeUpdate("upsert into user values
        (2,'Eva','Peters')");
        connection.commit();

        // Query for selecting records from table
        ps = connection.prepareStatement("select * from
        user");
        rs = ps.executeQuery();
        System.out.println("Table Values");
        while (rs.next()) {
                Integer id = rs.getInt(1);
                String name = rs.getString(2);
                System.out.println("\tRow: " + id + " = " +
                name);
        }
} catch (SQLException | ClassNotFoundException e) {
        e.printStackTrace();
} finally {
        if (ps != null) {
                try {
                        ps.close();
                } catch (Exception e) {
                }
        }
        if (rs != null) {
                try {
                        rs.close();
```

```
                            } catch (Exception e) {
                            }
                }
                if (statement != null) {
                        try {
                                statement.close();
                        } catch (Exception e) {
                        }
                }
                if (connection != null) {
                        try {
                                connection.close();
                        } catch (Exception e) {
                        }
                }
        }

    }
}
```

In PhoenixJdbc souce code listing you see traditional JDBC imports. This is because phoenix provide a JDBC driver for intracting with HBase. You can also mix existing JDBC apis with phoenix for your task wherever they required. The above listing code first creates a database connection by passing **jdbc: phoenix:localhost** as the JDBC URL to the **DriverManager** class. Just like in the phoenix cli console, localhost refers to the server running Zookeeper. If you were connecting to a production HBase instance, you would want to use server name or IP address for that production instance. The code itself explainatory and easy to understand if you already used JDBC programming.

The steps are as follows:

1. Create a Statement for the connection.

2. Execute statements using the executeUpdate () method.

3. Create a PreparedStatement to select inserted data.

4. Execute the PreparedStatement, retrieve a ResultSet, and iterate over the results.

You can build project by executing maven goal mvn clean install. To run this program your HBase server should be up and running. Go to your target directory and execute following command with your project created jar.

```
java -jar <your project jar>
```

For this project our jar will be phoenix-jdbc-1.0-SNAPSHOT.jar

3.7 Summary

In this chapter we discussed Phoenix basic commands, their syntax, and hands-on working examples. The main purpose was to get an idea of the available Phoenix data types and to set the context for upcoming chapters. This chapter just scratched the surface, demonstrating how easy it is to perform CRUD operations with Phoenix. Subsequent chapters will take a deep dive into the syntax of the various commands and show how Phoenix internally maps SQL commands to HBase operations.

CHAPTER 4

Querying Data

In the previous chapter, we discussed basic Phoenix commands for CRUD operations. In this chapter we will be digging deep into working with tables (creating, altering, and dropping tables), Phoenix available clauses (LIMIT, WHERE, GROUP BY, HAVING, and ORDER BY), data constraints (NOT NULL) and conditional operators (AND, OR, IN, LIKE, and BETWEEN) for data retrieval.

4.1   Constraints

Constraints are rules applied on the values, structure or result set. You can enforce constraints on columns and tables, such as PRIMARY KEY, that will enforce constraints while queries are conducted.

4.1.1   NOT NULL

The NOT NULL constraint enforces a column to NOT accept NULL values.

It enforces a field to always contain a value. This means that you cannot insert a new record, or update a record without adding a value to this field. Phoenix do not allow not null constraint on non-primary key columns.

The following SQL enforces the "CUST_ID" column and the "LNAME" column to not accept NULL values.

Syntax:

```
CREATE TABLE CUSTOMER
(
CUST_ID INTEGER NOT NULL,
FNAME VARCHAR,
LNAME VARCHAR NOT NULL,
EMAIL VARCHAR,
DOB DATE
CONSTRAINTS PRIMARY KEY(CUST_ID,LNAME))
```

© Shakil Akhtar and Ravi Magham 2017
S. Akhtar and R. Magham, *Pro Apache Phoenix*, DOI 10.1007/978-1-4842-2370-3_4

4.2 Creating Tables

CREATE TABLE follows SQL conventions, but the Phoenix version offers significant extensions to support a wide range of flexibility, including where the data files for tables are stored and the formats used.

CREATE TABLE creates a new table, and any column families referenced are created if they don't exist. By default, Table names, column family and column names are uppercased, but if you want to maintain case sensitivity for names then specify names inside double quotes. If any column family is available in HBase but is not listed, then that will be ignored. While creating a table, an empty key value is added to the first column family of any existing rows or to the default column family, which improves query performance. This is because having a key value column always guarantee to be there and minimize the amount of data that must be projected and subsequently returned back to the client.

■ **Note** An empty Key value is required because on deletion of all, columns will not remove the row key so that row columns can be queried.

Phoenix stores all the metadata of all tables in the HBase SYSTEM_CATALOG table. The parameter phoenix.schema.dropMetaData can be set to true or false for dropping the actual physical HBase table. It determines whether table needs to be dropped for HBase or not. If set to true, it will drop the HBase table. Setting this to false will delete the cells at the latest timestamp and retain the HBase table for back queries.

See how you can write syntax for creating tables:

CREATE TABLE schema.table_name (column1, column2...column(n))
CREATE TABLE "case_sensitive_table" (column1, column2... column(n))

The DDL will create a table with the given table_name having the specified number of columns and any constraints applied on them.

Example -

CREATE TABLE dbschema.CUSTOMER(CUST_ID BIGINT NOT NULL, FNAME VARCHAR (30), LNAME VARCHAR (30), EMAIL VARCHAR(50),DOB DATE CONSTRAINT PRIMARY KEY(CUST_ID))

CREATE TABLE table_name (ORDER_ID **bigint** NOT NULL primary key desc, ORDER_
DATE DATE , AMOUNT **DECIMAL**, quantity bigint)
DATA_BLOCK_ENCODING='DIFF'

IF NOT EXISTS while creating tables-

When using the **IF NOT EXISTS** clause, if a table already exists, then no change will be made to it, and no validation is done to check whether the existing table metadata matches the proposed table metadata.

So it's better to use DROP TABLE followed by **CREATE TABLE** if the table metadata may be changing.

Following syntax is for creating a table using IF NOT EXISTS clause:

```
CREATE TABLE IF NOT EXISTS "case_sensitive_table (column1 datatype, column2
datatype, ...column data type)
DATA_BLOCK_ENCODING='NONE', VERSIONS=5,
MAX_FILESIZE=2000000 split on (?, ?, ?)


CREATE TABLE IF NOT EXISTS schema_name. table_name (
ORDER_ID BIGINT, CUST_ID BIGINT, AMOUNT DECIMAL,
CONSTRAINT pk PRIMARY KEY (ORDER_ID, CUST_ID)) TTL=86400

0: jdbc:phoenix:localhost:2181:/hbase> CREATE TABLE IF NOT EXISTS
ORDERS(ORDER_ID BIGINT NOT NULL,ORDER_DATE DATE,CUST_ID BIGINT NOT NULL,
AMOUNT DECIMAL,QUANTITY BIGINT CONSTRAINT PK PRIMARY KEY (ORDER_ID,CUST_ID));
No rows affected (1.389 seconds)
```

```
0: jdbc:phoenix:localhost:2181:/hbase> !tables
```

TABLE_CAT	TABLE_SCHEM	TABLE_NAME
	SYSTEM	CATALOG
	SYSTEM	FUNCTION
	SYSTEM	SEQUENCE
	SYSTEM	STATS
		CUSTOMER
		ORDERS

After creating tables, use DESCRIBE TABLE to see that the database has created structure, columns, and column types. The following line describes the ORDERS table.

```
0: jdbc:phoenix:localhost> ! describe ORDERS
```

```
0: jdbc:phoenix:localhost:2181:/hbase> |describe orders
```

TABLE_CAT	TABLE_SCHEM	TABLE_NAME	COLUMN_NAME
		ORDERS	ORDER_ID
		ORDERS	ORDER_DATE
		ORDERS	CUST_ID
		ORDERS	AMOUNT
		ORDERS	QUANTITY

4.3 Salted Tables

HBase sequential write may suffer from region server hot spotting if the row key is monotonically increasing. To overcome this problem, salting can be used with row key. Salting can significantly increase performance by pre-splitting the data into multiple regions and avoiding sequential scan. Sequential scans are not always bad, and may sometimes even be good for certain use cases.

Salted tables do not store data in sequential fashion so results are returned naturally unsorted. Any queries that ask for ordering will have to force sequential table scan and decreases performance. You can also enforce ordering by adding the configuration property `phoenix.query.force.rowkeyorder`. This brings some performance degradation due to merge sort at the client but if query already contains order by and group by then it will not much affect performance.Uniform load distribution brings optimized write and also increases read queries performance.

In Phoenix, we can salt the row key with a salting byte for a table. This table option is known as SALT_BUCKETS and needs to be provided when creating table having a value from 1 to 256. When specified, Phoenix would pre-split the table in regions equal to the number of SALT_BUCKETS and each region start key prefix with the salt bytes to ensure even load distribution among region servers if the user does not provide any split point.

Syntax:

```
CREATE TABLE table (key VARCHAR PRIMARY KEY, column(n) data type(s)) SALT_
BUCKETS = number;
CREATE TABLE ORDERS (ORDER_ID BIGINT NOT NULL PRIMARY KEY, ORDER_NO BIGINT,
ORDER_DATE DATE) SALT_BUCKETS=10
```

In pre-split salting will be done automatically for tables but in case you want to exactly control where table split occurs without adding extra byte or change row key order then you can pre-split a table.

```
CREATE TABLE CUSTOMER (CUST_ID BIGINT NOT NULL PRIMARY KEY, FNAME VARCHAR,
LNAME VARCHAR , STATE VARCHAR,) SPLIT ON ('AZ','CA','NJ')
```

Creating table with column families--

Phoenix allows you to create a table with column families as supported by HBase. Column families are useful when we use a query to select some common columns and group them together. It improves performance at read time because with column families, related data is stored in separate files.

Syntax:

```
CREATE TABLE table_name (key primary key, A.column1 datatype, A.column2 data
type, B.column3 datatype)
```

In above create table DDL two column families, A and B, will be created.

```
0: jdbc:phoenix:localhost:2181:/hbase> CREATE TABLE ITEM (ITEM_ID VARCHAR NOT
NULL PRIMARY KEY, A.ITEM_CODE VARCHAR, A.ITEM_TYPE VARCHAR, B.PRICE DOUBLE);
No rows affected (1.386 seconds)
```

0: jdbc:phoenix:localhost:2181:/hbase> !describe ITEM

TABLE_CAT	TABLE_SCHEM	TABLE_NAME	COLUMN_NAME
		ITEM	ITEM_ID
		ITEM	ITEM_CODE
		ITEM	ITEM_TYPE
		ITEM	PRICE

It is important to consider performance while creating the table itself, as later it's hard to migrate or drop a table loaded with lots of data. Phoenix also gives ability for compression on disk that significantly improves performance on large tables.

To enable compression, you have to supply COMPRESSION parameter and its type while creating table.

Syntax:

```
CREATE TABLE table_name (Key data type PRIMARY KEY, column(s) data type(s))
COMPRESSION='compression type'
```

```
0: jdbc:phoenix:localhost:2181:/hbase> CREATE TABLE ITEM (ITEM_ID VARCHAR
NOT NULL PRIMARY KEY, A.ITEM_CODE VARCHAR, A.ITEM_TYPE VARCHAR, B.PRICE DOUBLE)
COMPRESSION='GZ';
```

4.4 Dropping Tables

The favorite DROP TABLE command from SQL is supported:

```
DROP TABLE IF EXISTS ORDERS
```

The **IF EXISTS** keywords are optional. It is used to ensure if table doesn't exist Phoenix should not return an error. On dropping a table, by default underlying HBase data and index tables are dropped as well. You can use property phoenix.*schema. dropMetaData* to override this and keep the HBase table for point-in-time queries.

■ **Note** An optional **CASCADE** keyword can be used to drop any available views for the table. This is used to drop dangling views for dropped tables. A table cannot be dropped if a view exists on the table.

Syntax:

```
DROP TABLE schema_name.table_name CASCADE;
```

4.5 ALTER Tables

A table alteration is required for modifying column adding new columns or deleting column from the table etc. In the section below adding, deleting column from table is explained.

4.5.1   Adding Columns

Adding column can be done by using keyword ADD followed by column name and data type. It is required to alter table for adding columns to it. We can use **ALTER TABLE** command as mentioned above.

Syntax:

```
ALTER TABLE table_name DROP column_name data type
```

```
ALTER TABLE CUSTOMER ADD PHONE_NO INTEGER (10);
```

```
0: jdbc:phoenix:localhost:2181:/hbase> ALTER TABLE CUSTOMER ADD PHONE_NO
INTEGER (10);
No rows affected (6.01 seconds)
```

Now you can query on the added column, and it can be added as a part of SELECT.

```
0: jdbc:phoenix:localhost:2181:/hbase> SELECT CUST_ID,PHONE_NO FROM CUSTOMER;
```

4.5.2   Deleting or Replacing Columns

Dropping a column is easy with using keyword DROP and COLUMN along with column name to be dropped. When this DDL statement executes a full table scan is performed and add delete marker to it

Syntax:

```
ALTER TABLE table_name DROP COLUMN column_name;
```

```
ALTER TABLE CUSTOMER DROP COLUMN PHONE_NO
```

In the example PHONE_NO column if exists will be dropped otherwise it will show an error if the column does not exist.

```
0: jdbc:phoenix:localhost:2181:/hbase> ALTER TABLE CUSTOMER DROP COLUMN PHONE_NO;
6 rows affected (0.022 seconds)
```

TABLE_NAME	COLUMN_NAME
CUSTOMER	CUST_ID
CUSTOMER	FNAME
CUSTOMER	LNAME
CUSTOMER	DOB
CUSTOMER	CITY
CUSTOMER	STATE

4.5.3   Renaming a Column

Renaming column or changing data type of a column command is not available in phoenix as a single command but there is way to achieve this. You first need to drop a column and then create a new column. What about the data if available in the column? Do we lose or it can be retained? If you have existing data, following steps can be used to retain it.

1. Create a new column (with the new name and possibly new type).

2. Run an **UPSERT SELECT** statement to copy migrate data from the old column to the new column. We will discuss **UPSERT** and **SELECT** in detail in querying part.

3. Drop the old column.

■ **Note**   The above operations can be slow depending upon the data available in the table, as it has to go two full table scans, once for UPSERT SELECT and other for dropping the column.

4.6   Clauses
4.6.1   LIMIT

While SELECT clauses select columns, LIMIT clauses are filters; a LIMIT clause can be used to specify the number of records to return. For example, if we write LIMIT 2, only two rows will be returned in the query result, provided the table has two or more than two records. The LIMIT clause can be very useful on large tables with millions of records, as returning a large number of records can impact on performance.

Let's use this clause in our retail orders table example.
Syntax:

```
0: jdbc:phoenix:localhost:2181:/hbase> SELECT * FROM ORDERS LIMIT 2;
```

4.6.2   WHERE

While SELECT clauses select columns, WHERE clauses are filters.

WHERE clauses use predicate expressions, applying predicate operators, which we'll describe in a moment, to columns. Several predicate expressions can be joined with AND and OR operators. When the predicate expressions evaluate to true, the corresponding rows are retained in the output.

```
0: jdbc:phoenix:localhost:2181:/hbase> SELECT * FROM ORDERS WHERE ORDER_ID=10249;
```

4.6.3   GROUP BY

The GROUP BY clause is used to arrange data into groups with aggregate functions. It is normally used in conjunction with SELECT.

```
SELECT column, aggregate_function(column)
FROM table
WHERE column operator value
GROUP BY column;
```

```
0: jdbc:phoenix:localhost:2181:/hbase> SELECT CUST_ID,SUM(QUANTITY) FROM
ORDERS GROUP BY CUST_ID;
```

```
0: jdbc:phoenix:localhost:2181:/hbase> SELECT CUST_ID,SUM(QUANTITY) FROM ORDERS GROUP BY CUST_ID;
+-------------------------------+-------------------------------+
|              CUST_ID          |           SUM(QUANTITY)       |
+-------------------------------+-------------------------------+
| 101                           | 40                            |
| 104                           | 20                            |
+-------------------------------+-------------------------------+
2 rows selected (0.014 seconds)
```

4.6.4   HAVING

The WHERE clause cannot be used for applying conditions on aggregate functions, so HAVING clause is introduced to support conditions on aggregate functions.

```
SELECT column1,
aggregate_function(column2)
FROM table(s)
GROUP BY column(s)
HAVING condition;
```

0: jdbc:phoenix:localhost:2181:/hbase> SELECT CUST_ID,SUM(QUANTITY) FROM ORDERS GROUP BY CUST_ID HAVING CUST_ID >101 ;

```
0: jdbc:phoenix:localhost:2181:/hbase> SELECT CUST_ID,SUM(QUANTITY) FROM ORDERS GROUP BY CUST_ID HAVING CUST_ID >101 ;
+------------------------------+------------------------------+
|             CUST_ID          |          SUM(QUANTITY)       |
+------------------------------+------------------------------+
| 104                          | 20                           |
+------------------------------+------------------------------+
1 row selected (0.02 seconds)
```

4.6.5   ORDER BY

This clause is used to sort the result set in ascending (ASC) or descending (DESC) order. By default, result set is sorted in ascending order.

```
SELECT column(s)
FROM table
ORDER BY column ASC|DESC, column ASC|DESC;
```

0: jdbc:phoenix:localhost:2181:/hbase> SELECT ORDER_ID,ORDER_DATE,CUST_ID FROM ORDERS ORDER BY ORDER_DATE ASC;

```
|0: jdbc:phoenix:localhost:2181:/hbase> SELECT ORDER_ID,ORDER_DATE,CUST_ID FROM ORDERS ORDER BY ORDER_DATE ASC;
+------------------------+------------------------------+------------------------+
|        ORDER_ID        |          ORDER_DATE          |        CUST_ID         |
+------------------------+------------------------------+------------------------+
| 10248                  | 1998-04-07 00:00:00.000 | 101                      |
| 10249                  | 1998-05-07 00:00:00.000 | 101                      |
| 10301                  | 1998-06-07 00:00:00.000 | 101                      |
| 10444                  | 1998-08-07 00:00:00.000 | 104                      |
| 10340                  | 1998-10-10 00:00:00.000 | 104                      |
+------------------------+------------------------------+------------------------+
5 rows selected (0.021 seconds)
```

0: jdbc:phoenix:localhost:2181:/hbase> SELECT ORDER_ID,ORDER_DATE,CUST_ID FROM ORDERS ORDER BY ORDER_ID DESC;

```
|0: jdbc:phoenix:localhost:2181:/hbase> SELECT ORDER_ID,ORDER_DATE,CUST_ID FROM ORDERS ORDER BY ORDER_ID DESC;
+------------------------+------------------------------+------------------------+
|        ORDER_ID        |          ORDER_DATE          |        CUST_ID         |
+------------------------+------------------------------+------------------------+
| 10444                  | 1998-08-07 00:00:00.000 | 104                      |
| 10340                  | 1998-10-10 00:00:00.000 | 104                      |
| 10301                  | 1998-06-07 00:00:00.000 | 101                      |
| 10249                  | 1998-05-07 00:00:00.000 | 101                      |
| 10248                  | 1998-04-07 00:00:00.000 | 101                      |
+------------------------+------------------------------+------------------------+
5 rows selected (0.021 seconds)
```

4.7 Logical Operators

4.7.1 AND

The AND operator displays a record if both the first condition AND the second condition are true

```
0: jdbc:phoenix:localhost:2181:/hbase> SELECT CUST_ID,FNAME,CITY,STATE FROM
CUSTOMER WHERE CUST_ID >100 AND STATE='Texas';
```

4.7.2 OR

The OR operator displays a record if either the first condition OR the second condition is true.

```
0: jdbc:phoenix:localhost:2181:/hbase> SELECT CUST_ID,FNAME,CITY,STATE FROM
CUSTOMER WHERE CUST_ID >200 OR STATE='Arizona';
```

4.7.3 IN

The IN operator displays a record if the first item can be found in a specified list.

```
SELECT column(s)
FROM table
WHERE column IN (value1,value2,...);
```

```
0: jdbc:phoenix:localhost:2181:/hbase> SELECT CUST_ID,FNAME,CITY,STATE FROM
CUSTOMER WHERE STATE IN ('Arizona','Texas');
```

4.7.4   LIKE

Use the LIKE operator in WHERE clause to search for a specific pattern.
   Syntax:

```
SELECT column(s)
FROM table
WHERE column LIKE pattern;
```

0: jdbc:phoenix:localhost:2181:/hbase> SELECT CUST_ID,FNAME,CITY,STATE FROM CUSTOMER WHERE STATE LIKE 'Tex%';

4.7.5   BETWEEN

BETWEEN is used for range selection. It does an inclusive comparison for both operands.

```
SELECT column(s)
FROM table
WHERE column BETWEEN value1 AND value2;
```

0: jdbc:phoenix:localhost:2181:/hbase> SELECT ORDER_ID, ORDER_DATE, CUST_ID FROM ORDERS WHERE ORDER_ID BETWEEN 10300 AND 10400;

4.8   Summary

In this chapter we discussed phoenix building blocks and its available constructs for general query writing on HBase data store. You have seen how to work with tables, constraints, clauses and their available types. These are primary things we should be knowing while working with SQL. Although Structured Query Language (SQL) supports variety of ways to write queries and more feature rich than phoenix querying to HBase data. The reason is RDBMS are stabilized and less flexible than NoSQL databases and phoenix team did a great job in providing many out of the box features considering data performance in mind.

CHAPTER 5

■ ■ ■

Advanced Querying

Chapter 4 discussed more on generic querying where only one table is involved.
We saw how to restrict values using constraints, a go through on table concepts and use
of operators in phoenix query language. In chapter 5, we will look into more advanced
querying like SQL joins, filters on the result set using subqueries and working with
multiple tables. Let's see how these advanced concepts work and their use in phoenix.

5.1   Joins

In general querying, we saw how to work with single table. Now let's explore how to work
with multiple tables. When we want to retrieve data from more than one tables from
database, joins are used to collect required columns data in a single query. Joins are
heavy and slower than plain queries but phoenix supports many configurations and hints
to fine tune your join query performance for faster results. We will discuss them in this
chapter while explaining join optimizations section.

Let's see how we can write a join query in Phoenix with an example.

```
0: jdbc:phoenix:localhost:2181:/hbase> SELECT O.ORDER_ID, C.FNAME,C.CITY,
O.ORDER_DATE FROM ORDERS AS O,CUSTOMER AS C WHERE O.CUST_ID = C.CUST_ID;
```

5.2   Inner Join

This is most frequently used join type also known as EQUIJOIN. Inner join returns all
rows from tables where the matching key records of one table is equal to the key records
of another table (see Figure 5-1).

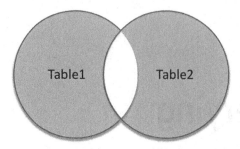

Figure 5-1. *Inner Join*

Consider our example where we have a Customer table and an Orders table. If we search how many customers placed orders and on what date, then a join will be used on Customer and Orders tables to find aggregate results. Following is the join query to find these results.

Syntax:

```
SELECT t1.column1, t2.column2...
FROM table1 t1
INNER JOIN table2 t2
ON t1.column = t2.column;
```

```
0: jdbc:phoenix:localhost:2181:/hbase> SELECT O.ORDER_ID, C.FNAME,C.CITY,
O.ORDER_DATE FROM ORDERS AS O INNER JOIN CUSTOMER AS C ON O.CUST_ID = C.CUST_ID;
```

```
0: jdbc:phoenix:localhost:2181:/hbase> SELECT O.ORDER_ID, C.FNAME,C.CITY, O.ORDER_DATE FROM ORDERS AS O INNER JOIN CUSTOMER AS C ON O.CUST_ID = C.CUST_ID;
+------------+------------------+------------------+--------------------------+
|  O.ORDER_ID |       C.FNAME    |      C.CITY       |        O.ORDER_DATE      |
+------------+------------------+------------------+--------------------------+
| 10248      | Donald           | Nogales          | 1998-04-07 00:00:00.000  |
| 10249      | Donald           | Nogales          | 1998-05-07 00:00:00.000  |
| 10301      | Donald           | Nogales          | 1998-06-07 00:00:00.000  |
| 10340      | John             | Los Angeles      | 1998-10-10 00:00:00.000  |
| 10444      | John             | Los Angeles      | 1998-08-07 00:00:00.000  |
+------------+------------------+------------------+--------------------------+
5 rows selected (0.029 seconds)
```

5.3   Outer Join

Just like in SQL, an OUTER JOIN in Phoenix returns all records from the participating tables which satisfy the join condition along with records which do not satisfy the condition. It has two subtypes LEFT OUTER JOIN or LEFT JOIN and RIGHT OUTER JOIN or RIGHT JOIN. Following section describes these two subtypes with examples.

5.3.1   Left Outer Join

LEFT OUTER JOIN or LEFT JOIN returns all records from the left-side table, even if there are no matching records from the right-side table. This means if the condition is not matched in the right table, the join will still return records in the result having null in each column. See Figure 5-2 for a left join pictorial representation (See *Figure 5-2. Left Join*).

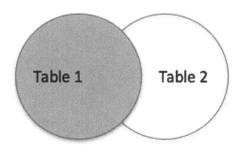

Figure 5-2. *Left Join*

Syntax:

```
SELECT t1.column1, t2.column2...
FROM table1 t1
LEFT JOIN table2 t2
ON t1.column = t2.column;
```

0: jdbc:phoenix:localhost:2181:/hbase> SELECT O.ORDER_ID, C.LNAME,C.CITY,
O.ORDER_DATE FROM ORDERS O LEFT OUTER JOIN CUSTOMER C ON O.CUST_ID = C.CUST_ID;

0: jdbc:phoenix:localhost:2181:/hbase> SELECT O.ORDER_ID, C.LNAME,C.CITY,
O.ORDER_DATE FROM ORDERS O LEFT JOIN CUSTOMER C ON O.CUST_ID = C.CUST_ID;

5.3.2 Right Outer Join

RIGHT OUTER JOIN or RIGHT JOIN returns all records from the right-side table even if there are no matching records from the left-side table. This means if the condition is not matched in the left table, the join will still return records in the result having null in each column. See *Figure 5-3. Right Join*) for right join pictorial representation.

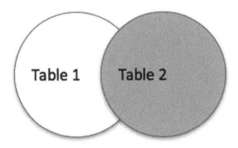

Figure 5-3. *Right Join*

Syntax:

```
SELECT t1.column1, t2.column2...
FROM table1 t1
RIGHT JOIN table2 t2
ON t1.column = t2.column;
```

0: jdbc:phoenix:localhost:2181:/hbase> SELECT O.ORDER_ID, C.FNAME, C.CITY, O.ORDER_DATE FROM ORDERS O RIGHT OUTER JOIN CUSTOMER C ON O.CUST_ID = C.CUST_ID;

0: jdbc:phoenix:localhost:2181:/hbase> SELECT O.ORDER_ID, C.FNAME, C.CITY, O.ORDER_DATE FROM ORDERS O RIGHT JOIN CUSTOMER C ON O.CUST_ID = C.CUST_ID;

5.3.3 Full Outer Join

This type of join returns all rows from both the left-side table and the right-side table. If there are missing entries, it will add null to them. It is basically combined result of both left and right joins. In Figure (Figure 5-4), Table 1 is the left-side table and Table 2 is the right-side table.

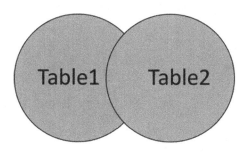

Figure 5-4. *Full Join*

Syntax:

```
SELECT t1.column1, t2.column2...
FROM table1 t1
FULL JOIN table2 t2
ON t1.column = t2.column;
```

0: jdbc:phoenix:localhost:2181:/hbase> SELECT O.ORDER_ID, C.FNAME, C.LNAME, O.ORDER_DATE FROM ORDERS O FULL OUTER JOIN CUSTOMER C ON O.CUST_ID = C.CUST_ID;

0: jdbc:phoenix:localhost:2181:/hbase> SELECT O.ORDER_ID, C.FNAME, C.LNAME, O.ORDER_DATE FROM ORDERS O FULL JOIN CUSTOMER C ON O.CUST_ID = C.CUST_ID;

5.4   Grouped Joins

Group joins, also known as subjoins, are complex nested join queries. Phoenix has support of group join for handling complex joins. These joins are normally applied on outer and inner joins where inner query joins results further as nested query joins. Here one thing is to be noted about phoenix nested joins, they are always surrounded by parenthesis in query.

Syntax:

```
SELECT t1.column1, t2.column2,t3.column...
FROM table1 t1
Join1
    (table2 t2
     join2 table3 t3
     ON t2.column = t3.column)
ON t1.column = t2.column;
```

```
0: jdbc:phoenix:localhost:2181:/hbase> SELECT O.ORDER_ID, I.ITEM_ID,
S.SUPPLIER_NAME,S.CITY FROM ORDERS AS O LEFT JOIN (ITEM AS I INNER JOIN
SUPPLIER AS S ON I.SUPPLIER_ID = S.SUPPLIER_ID) ON O.ITEM_ID = I.ITEM_ID;
```

5.5 Hash Join

Phoenix internally uses hash and merge joins for join operations. In Hash join phoenix computes the results for the RHS of a join condition and broadcasts the results onto all the RS of HBase. Data is cached and data cache age can be configured by using phoenix. coprocessor.maxServerCacheTimeToLiveMs property which allows increasing the cache time on the server. The sequence of steps followed for Hash Join are:

1. The Phoenix client executes the RHS of the join query given by client.

2. The results returned are serialized and broadcasted to all RS which hold the regions of the LHS table using HBase Endpoint Coprocessors.

3. Since endpoint coprocessors are primarily RPC services which follow the request / response pattern using Protocol Buffers, the servers cache the serialized data onto the server and respond with an acknowledgement.

4. The Phoenix client then triggers the execution of the LHS of the join query.

5. On the server end, since the RHS of the data is resident in memory, the join is done and the results are returned.

6. Once the join query is complete, the client then triggers another RPC call to free up the serve cache on the region servers.

5.6   Sort Merge Join

This join is preferred mostly for the cases where Hash Join doesn't scale and work. Its suggested to use sort-merge join where the results of both LHS and RHS are sorted and the merge happens on the client side.

5.7   Join Query Optimizations

As we know from SQL, joins are slow because of huge relation data sets that often require complete table scans. Phoenix automatically performs many optimizations for us when we execute any join query. For example, Phoenix uses secondary indexes, if defined in the table, to improve performance. (We will see more on indexes in coming chapters.) It is important to understand that at least one table must be of a size that can fit into memory for Hash Joins, while sort merge join relations can be of any size. If you run into memory problems with very large tables, then allocate enough memory to Phoenix by changing configuration settings.

You can use hints to tell the query engine which join algorithm should be used. By default, Phoenix uses Hash Join algorithm whenever possible, because these are faster than any other join algorithms. If you want to use another join algorithm, such as a sort merge, then pass an attribute like USE_SORT_MERGE_JOIN in the query hint that will be enforced while executing the query internally. Although we can use algorithms as per need, it is suggested to use the Hash Join algorithm when one of the relations or result sets of table fits into memory, otherwise use a Sort Merge Join algorithm for faster results.

Two more options NO_STAR_JOIN and NO_CHILD_PARENT_JOIN_ OPTIMIZATION, are available as join hints. The NO_STAR_JOIN is used to tell the optimizer not to use a star join query to broadcast querying results for one common table to all region servers. Similarly, you can use other options to instruct the optimizer not to do point lookups between a child and a parent table for a correlated subquery.

See the following example where CUSTOMER and ORDERS are used in the joins section after using a hint to enforce the join algorithm.

```
0: jdbc:phoenix:localhost:2181:/hbase> EXPLAIN SELECT /*+USE_SORT_MERGE_
JOIN*/O.ORDER_ID, C.FNAME, C.LNAME,C.CITY, O.ORDER_DATE FROM ORDERS AS O
INNER JOIN CUSTOMER AS C ON O.CUST_ID = C.CUST_ID;
```

While looking at the query plan, it shows enforced self-merge-join as join algorithm.

```
0: jdbc:phoenix:localhost:2181:/hbase> EXPLAIN SELECT /*+USE_SORT_MERGE_JOIN*/O.ORDER_ID, C.FNAME, C.LNAME,C.CITY, O.ORDER_DATE FROM ORDERS AS O INNER JOIN CUSTOMER AS C ON O.CUST_ID = C.CUST_ID;
+-----------------------------------------------------+
|                        PLAN                         |
+-----------------------------------------------------+
| SORT-MERGE-JOIN (INNER) TABLES                      |
|     CLIENT 1-CHUNK PARALLEL 1-WAY FULL SCAN OVER ORDERS |
|         SERVER SORTED BY [O.CUST_ID]                |
|     CLIENT MERGE SORT                               |
| AND                                                 |
|     CLIENT 1-CHUNK PARALLEL 1-WAY FULL SCAN OVER CUSTOMER |
+-----------------------------------------------------+
```

If we don't define a hint, then default join algorithm will be used.

```
0: jdbc:phoenix:localhost:2181:/hbase> EXPLAIN SELECT O.ORDER_ID, C.FNAME, C.LNAME,C.CITY, O.ORDER_DATE FROM ORDERS AS O INNER JOIN CUSTOMER AS C ON O.CUST_ID = C.CUST_ID;
+-----------------------------------------------------+
|                        PLAN                         |
+-----------------------------------------------------+
| CLIENT 1-CHUNK PARALLEL 1-WAY FULL SCAN OVER ORDERS |
|     PARALLEL INNER-JOIN TABLE 0                     |
|         CLIENT 1-CHUNK PARALLEL 1-WAY FULL SCAN OVER CUSTOMER |
+-----------------------------------------------------+
3 rows selected (0.007 seconds)
```

5.7.1   Optimizing Through Configuration Properties

Cache has been primary technology to improve significant performance while working
with databases. Same fundamentals are applied here in phoenix for HBase querying.
Phoenix coprocessors do lot of work on server to give response time in seconds, while at
the same time aggregating results by working with region server caches. It is important to
set significant cache memory for relations data on servers. Phoenix builds hash table on
region server for smaller relations. These relations can be physical table, views, subqueries
or a join results. Underlying configuration properties can be tweaked to improve query
performance. You can define these properties in `hbase-site.xml`. If HBase is already
running, then region server restart is required to take effect of these properties.

> *phoenix.query.maxServerCacheBytes*: defines the
> maximum raw results size that can be compressed and
> sent to the region servers. If the size is exceeded, it will throw
> `MaxServerCacheSizeExceededException`. By default, memory
> bytes are 100 MB.

> *phoenix.query.maxGlobalMemoryPercentage:* This property
> shows the percentage of total available heap memory.
> The sum of all working caches must be less than this
> global memory pool size; if not, you might encounter
> `InsufficientMemoryException`. As a default, 15 percent is
> taken for global memory.

> *phoenix.coprocessor.maxServerCacheTimeToLiveMs:* This
> property defines the maximum server cache living time in
> milliseconds. A cache entry will be removed after spending
> this much idle time. Default time is set to 30,000 milliseconds.

5.7.2   Optimizing Query

As a hash join requires more memory, it is important to know which part of the join query
(left or right part) commonly taken as a smaller relation and stored on server cache.
Table 5-1. *Join types and their cache storage* explains the general behaviour.

Table 5-1. *Join types and their cache storage*

Join Type	relation cache storage
left side INNER JOIN right side	right side of INNER JOIN will be built as a hash table in server cache
left side LEFT JOIN/LEFT OUTER JOIN right side	right side of LEFT JOIN/LEFT OUTER JOIN will be built as a hash table in server cache
left side RIGHT JOIN/RIGHT OUTER JOIN right side	left side of RIGHT JOIN/RIGHT OUTER JOIN will be built as a hash table in server cache

If your query has multiple joins it is suggested to use EXPLAIN query plan and check what can be tuned in query to improve overall performance. You can also consider hints while tuning query after analyzing query execution plan.

5.8   Subqueries

A Phoenix subquery or nested query is a query within another Phoenix query used within a WHERE clause as a condition to filter or restrict result data. Nested queries must be enclosed within parentheses.

Syntax:

```
SELECT column(s)
FROM   table(s)
WHERE  column OPERATOR
     (SELECT column(s)
     FROM table(s)
     [WHERE])
```

Now we have seen syntax for subquery, let's do an example on this. Consider our customer table where we want to search customers having date of birth (DOB) greater that conditional date. Here the query inside parenthesis is sub query to fetch customers with DOB greater than 1975-01-01. The outer query makes use of inner query (in parenthesis) returned results for matching criteria.

```
0: jdbc:phoenix:localhost:2181:/hbase>   SELECT CUST_ID,FNAME,LNAME,DOB
FROM CUSTOMER WHERE CUST_ID IN (SELECT CUST_ID FROM CUSTOMER WHERE DOB >
to_date('1975-01-01'));
```

5.8.1   IN and NOT IN in Subqueries

We already discussed IN in Chapter 4. IN can be also used with subqueries in a WHERE clause. The following example shows how to write a query using these together.

Most of the time, Phoenix internally translates IN and NOT IN into semi-joins and anti-joins to get better performance out of it.

A semi-join differs from a conventional join as it returns rows at most once from the first table. Even if the second table contains many matches for the rows in the first table, only one copy will be returned.

An anti-join is opposite of a semi-join. While a semi-join returns matching rows from a table, an anti-join returns one copy of each row from the first table for which no match was found.

```
0: jdbc:phoenix:localhost:2181:/hbase>    SELECT ITEM_ID,ITEM_TYPE,PRICE
FROM ITEM WHERE ITEM_ID IN (SELECT ITEM_ID FROM ORDERS WHERE ORDER_DATE >=
to_date('1998-5-7'));
```

5.8.2   EXISTS and NOT EXISTS Clauses

In Chapter 4 we discussed many clauses in simple querying. EXISTS and NOT EXISTS are also clauses that used along with subqueries. They just check if any record returned by inner query (subquery) exists and return a Boolean TRUE otherwise FALSE.

Like IN and NOT IN phoenix translates EXISTS and NOT EXISTS into semi-joins and anti joins (see above section for semi and anti joins) to improve overall query performance.

```
0: jdbc:phoenix:localhost:2181:/hbase>    SELECT ITEM_ID,ITEM_TYPE,PRICE FROM
ITEM I WHERE EXISTS(SELECT * FROM ORDERS WHERE ORDER_DATE >= to_date('1998-5-7')
AND ITEM_ID=I.ITEM_ID);
```

Underlying query illustrates NOT EXISTS that will return rows not matching criteria.

```
0: jdbc:phoenix:localhost:2181:/hbase> SELECT C.CUST_ID,C.FNAME FROM CUSTOMER
C WHERE C.CUST_ID = 101 AND NOT EXISTS (SELECT * FROM ORDERS O WHERE O.ORDER_
DATE = to_date('1997-4-7') AND O.CUST_ID =C.CUST_ID)ORDER BY C.FNAME;
```

5.8.3 ANY, SOME, and ALL Operators with Subqueries

You can use comparison operators with subqueries to filter rows in the result set.
    Syntax:

```
SELECT column(s) | expression1
FROM table
WHERE expression2 operator {ALL | ANY | SOME} ( subquery )
```

The following query illustrates ANY comparison operator for the ORDERS table to
find maximum quantity of records.

```
0: jdbc:phoenix:localhost:2181:/hbase> SELECT ORDER_ID FROM ORDERS WHERE
QUANTITY >= ANY (SELECT max(QUANTITY) FROM ORDERS GROUP BY ITEM_ID);
```

Now let's do one query using an ALL operator with a subquery from ours Orders table.

```
0: jdbc:phoenix:localhost:2181:/hbase> SELECT ORDER_ID FROM ORDERS WHERE
QUANTITY >= ALL (SELECT max(QUANTITY) FROM ORDERS GROUP BY ITEM_ID);
```

5.8.4 UPSERT Using Subqueries

You can use subqueries with UPSERT statements for inserting data returned from
subqueries into another table. Consider a table backup of our existing CUSTOMER
table called CUST_BACKUP. We want to copy data from CUSTOMER to CUST_BACKUP.
Underlying query will do this work for us.

```
0: jdbc:phoenix:localhost:2181:/hbase> UPSERT INTO CUST_BACKUP SELECT * FROM
CUSTOMER WHERE CUST_ID IN (SELECT CUST_ID FROM CUSTOMER);
```

73

```
0: jdbc:phoenix:localhost:2181:/hbase> UPSERT INTO CUST_BACKUP SELECT * FROM CUSTOMER WHERE CUST_ID IN (SELECT CUST_ID FROM CUSTOMER);
6 rows affected (0.051 seconds)
0: jdbc:phoenix:localhost:2181:/hbase> SELECT * FROM CUST_BACKUP;
```

CUST_ID	FNAME	LNAME	DOB
100	John	Gray	1975-01-01 00:00:00.000
101	Donald	Duck	1980-02-05 00:00:00.000
102	Cindy	Hall	1990-04-01 00:00:00.000
103	Andrew	Hall	1975-03-05 00:00:00.000
104	John	Smith	1975-04-01 00:00:00.000
105	Lisa	John	1997-02-06 00:00:00.000

```
6 rows selected (0.039 seconds)
```

5.9   Views

Phoenix supports standard SQL views, with some limitations to it. In general, a view is just a SQL statement kept in the database having a name to it. A view is like a virtual table, having columns from one or more tables clubbed together. Although phoenix views inherit parent table columns but you can define additional columns to them. Phoenix allows these tables to share same underlying physical HBase table. As views share same HBase table, their size must be limited to give a reasonable performance to an extent (phoenix documentation says up to 100 tables). As the number grows, performance will be affected accordingly.

Currently Phoenix supports creating views for a single table and for all columns in the view creation, that is, SELECT *. Phoenix gives little relax on dropping non-primary key columns from table in the view.

While creating views if simple equity expressions are used then those views can be updated and known as Updatable Views. If there are more complex expressions, then updating views are not allowed and can be used for read only purpose. These types of views are known as Read-only views.

Let's see in following section how to create views and work with them.

5.9.1   Creating Views

A view can be created using the following syntax We can define new columns while creating view in the parenthesis.

Syntax:

```
CREATE VIEW view_name AS
SELECT column(s)
FROM table_name
WHERE [condition]
```

```
0: jdbc:phoenix:localhost:2181:/hbase> CREATE VIEW VIEW_HIGH_PRICE_ITEMS AS
SELECT *  FROM ITEM WHERE PRICE > 15;
```

ITEM_ID	ITEM_CODE	ITEM_TYPE	PRICE	
A1000	CH001	Clothing	20.28	8240
A1700	CH003	Food	50.0	8333
A3300	CH005	Clothing	199.0	8240

```
3 rows selected (0.025 seconds)
```

If you check the type of created view, this will show the type as 'VIEW'.

```
0: jdbc:phoenix:localhost:2181:/hbase> !table
```

TABLE_CAT	TABLE_SCHEM	TABLE_NAME	TABLE_TYP
	SYSTEM	CATALOG	SYSTEM TABLE
	SYSTEM	FUNCTION	SYSTEM TABLE
	SYSTEM	SEQUENCE	SYSTEM TABLE
	SYSTEM	STATS	SYSTEM TABLE
		CUSTOMER	TABLE
		ITEM	TABLE
		ORDERS	TABLE
		SUPPLIER	TABLE
		VIEW_HIGH_PRICE_ITEMS	VIEW

Let's see an example where we can add new columns to the view.

In the view VIEW_HIGH_PRICE_ITEMS, lets add one column for discontinued items. Before creating any column, running a query !describe VIEW_HIGH_PRICE_ITEMS will show only columns from parent table in the result. Now add one column and execute describe command that will display view having a newly added column in the view metadata.

```
0: jdbc:phoenix:localhost:2181:/hbase> CREATE VIEW VIEW_HIGH_PRICE_
ITEMS(HIGH_PRICE_ITEM DOUBLE) AS SELECT *  FROM ITEM WHERE PRICE > 15;
```

```
0: jdbc:phoenix:localhost:2181:/hbase> !describe  VIEW_HIGH_PRICE_ITEMS;
```

TABLE_CAT	TABLE_SCHEM	TABLE_NAME	COLUMN_NAME
		VIEW_HIGH_PRICE_ITEMS	ITEM_ID
		VIEW_HIGH_PRICE_ITEMS	ITEM_CODE
		VIEW_HIGH_PRICE_ITEMS	ITEM_TYPE
		VIEW_HIGH_PRICE_ITEMS	PRICE
		VIEW_HIGH_PRICE_ITEMS	SUPPLIER_ID
		VIEW_HIGH_PRICE_ITEMS	HIGH_PRICE_ITEM

5.9.2   Dropping Views

It uses similar syntax as dropping a table, just prefix the statement with the 'VIEW' attribute.

Syntax:

```
DROP VIEW view_name;
```

Now let's run a drop view command on our created view VIEW_HIGH_PRICE_ITEMS. After executing above command, you can validate view is removed from phoenix by running !tables command on the view.

```
0: jdbc:phoenix:localhost:2181:/hbase> DROP VIEW ITEMS_ABOVE_AVERAGE_PRICE;
No rows affected (0.019 seconds)
```

5.10   Paged Queries

Paging is very intuitive part for any web applications to give user seamless experience on web. If the query data is huge to show on the UI, application designer access records in pages limiting number of rows to get better data handling and performance. Although phoenix does not support paging in the way standard SQL support in query but phoenix has concept of page query that can be used to get similar sort of result. Phoenix allows paged queries with the help of Row Value Constructor(RVC) and Offset with limit. Let's see what are these and how we can use them for pagination.

5.10.1   LIMIT and OFFSET

To allow paging you can pair OFFSET with LIMIT. OFFSET defines a starting point and LIMIT sets the page size that tells Phoenix how many records to present in one page.
    Syntax:

```
SELECT column(s) FROM table
LIMIT value OFFSET value
```

For example, if we have a page size of 10 and want to retrieve a second page, the query will look like this:

```
SELECT ORDER_ID,ITEM_ID,QUANTITY FROM ORDERS WHERE ORDER_DATE > to_
date('1998-6-7') ORDER BY ORDER_ID LIMIT 10 OFFSET 10;
```

5.10.2   Row Value Constructor

A Row Value Constructor (RVC) is an ordered set of values enclosed within parentheses. This can be thought of as constructing a row with a series of values, just like a table row composed of fields and columns. Lets see how to query them with an example.
    Syntax:

```
(column1,column2....,column(n))

(8249,'ABC Corporation','Dayton')
('A1000','Clothing',20.28,8249)
```

You can use row value constructors in comparison expressions in a way similar to the use of regular values.

```
WHERE (LNAME,FNAME) =('Hall', 'Andrew')

WHERE(ITEM_ID,PRICE) >=(A1000,15)

0: jdbc:phoenix:localhost:2181:/hbase> SELECT * FROM CUSTOMER WHERE
(LNAME,FNAME)=('Hall','Andrew') ;
```

You can use row value constructor for stepping through set of rows. See the following query, that would move 5 rows at a time. Here client binds two variables to the values of the last row processed. The next invocation to it would find next 5 matching rows. This behaves like a page of pagination where we hope through page size.

```
0: jdbc:phoenix:localhost:2181:/hbase> SELECT ORDER_ID,ITEM_ID,QUANTITY
FROM ORDERS WHERE ORDER_DATE > to_date('1998-6-7') AND (ITEM_ID,QUANTITY)
>=('A1101',5) ORDER BY ORDER_ID LIMIT 5;
```

5.11   Summary

Phoenix supports complex querying on HBase data and can be customized for fast query results. When we deal with millions of rows of huge data, it is important to get reasonable performance. Phoenix caching configuration properties can help us improve performance and build faster relations on the server. We saw how to write complex queries using Phoenix joins, subqueries, and views for tables. Phoenix can be used for even more complex queries based on these fundamental concepts. In later chapters we will discuss indexes, transactions, and other important features that bolster Phoenix as a great choice for an SQL skin over HBase.

## CHAPTER 6

Transactions

When we discuss databases either Relations or Non-relational transactions are more important to ensure data integrity or dealing with concurrent tasks. Transactions also play an important role when handling database errors and avoiding database to any inconsistent state. Transactions are an integral part of relational databases. Although majority of NoSQL databases do not have full support for transactions but some of them provide transactions support with the help of a transaction manager. Similarly, HBase leverage Apache Tephra as the transaction manager for transactions support. In this chapter, we will see how Phoenix supports transactions.

6.1   SQL Transactions

A transaction is basically a process of one or more changes done in the database in a logical order. It can be done in a manual fashion by a user or automatically by a database program. Moreover, a transaction is a sequence of reads and writes. It is important to control transactions to ensure data integrity and to handle database errors. Practically, you will club SQL queries into a group and execute all of them together as a part of a transaction.

Consider an example of transferring an amount from one account to another, and how this can be grouped together in a transaction. The steps to be performed are:

> **Step1**: Read from account A
>
> **Step2**: Write to account A
>
> **Step3**: Read from account B
>
> **Step4**: Write to account B

6.2   Transaction Properties

A transaction is managed and monitored by a transaction manager, also called a transaction monitor, which ensures four primary attributes (properties) for any transaction. These are atomicity, consistency, isolation, and durability. In short, they are commonly called the ACID properties of a transaction.

6.2.1   Atomicity

Atomicity ensures all operations as a unit of work are committed at once. If a failure occurs, the transaction will be aborted, and any previous operations will roll back to their former state.

6.2.2   Consistency

Consistency makes sure that database changes will not be committed as a partial state change in the event of a failure. Changes should be saved only upon a successful transaction commit.

6.2.3   Isolation

Isolation allows multiple transactions to run independently of one another. Transactions run in their own allocated space and do not see each other's changes. A transaction is visible only after it is committed, thus avoiding "dirty reads" due to partial changes.

6.2.4   Durability

Durability ensures that committed transactions changes are stored permanently to the database and do not disappear or get erased, even if database crashes.

6.3   Transaction Control

Transactions are part of data consistency and failure handling in a relational database. The following commands are used to control transactions. These control commands are used with DML operations INSERT, UPDATE, and DELETE for relational databases.

6.3.1   COMMIT

After completing a transaction, COMMIT saves changes to the database. It makes sure that all data is synced and stored, and associated with current transaction.

6.3.2   ROLLBACK

A ROLLBACK can be performed following an error or a failure in a transaction to return the database its previous state, as it was before starting the transaction. It will not store any changes performed to the database during the rolled-back transaction.

6.3.3   SAVEPOINT

A SAVEPOINT is basically a state of the database that can be restored by a ROLLBACK. Let's take an example to understand save points. Imagine that you started a transaction or group of transactions from database state 'A.' After some changes or some transaction commits, the database came to state B and similar other states. You can revert your changes to these points (a.k.a. save points) or states. These points can be within groups of transactions in which to ROLLBACK.

6.3.4   SET TRANSACTION

You can give a name to a transaction using SET TRANSACTION. A transaction with a name is easy to read and find.

6.4   Transactions in HBase

NoSQL databases are meant for solving the problem of scalability and read-write performance and keep less focus on transactions but some NoSQL databases support transactions with the help of a transaction manager either inbuilt or integrating with a third-party transaction manager. HBase provides transaction support by using Apache Tephra as a transaction manager. Apache HBase does not completely support ACID properties, but it guarantees a good part of these for transactions. You can find more on HBase transactions support on their website `https://hbase.apache.org/acid-semantics.html`.

The rowkey also provides a logical grouping of cells; and HBase ensures that all cells with the same rowkey are co-located on the same server (called a Region Server in HBase), which allows for ACID guarantees for updates with the same rowkey without complicated and slow two-phase-commit or paxos.

HBase supports atomic operations for cell value and batch operations on rows within a region. The cell value atomicity is maintained by using `checkAndPut`, `checkAndDelete`, increment, append. HBase supports batch operations on rows for example cross row operations within region supports through `MultiRowMutationEndPoint`. It does not support cross-region, cross table and multi-RPC atomic operations.

As Phoenix is SQL skin over HBase, that means it also applies underlying HBase transaction limitations.

Before moving into phoenix transactions section let's have a look on Apache Tephra, a key part for allowing transaction capabilities.

6.4.1   Integrating HBase with Transaction Manager

By default, HBase does not provide full ACID support, but we can achieve a broader set of transaction features by integrating a third party transaction manager.

You can plug in a transaction manager and configure it either for single point failure or active and standby with high availability support. This transaction manager service will be registered with Zookeeper and a client, for example, Apache Phoenix might be used to start a transaction. Communications will occur among client, transaction manager, and the HBase region server. The interactions between these components are shown in Figure 6-1.

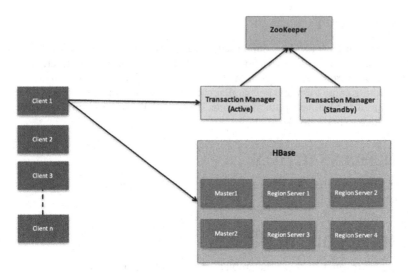

Figure 6-1. *HBase with Transaction Manager*

6.4.2 Components of Transaction Manager

The following components play mostly inside a third party transaction API like Apache Tephra. We will discuss them here to understand how transactions work inside HBase.

6.4.2.1 TransactionAware Client

A TransactionAware client coordinates the transaction lifecycle with the transaction manager and directly communicates with HBase for reads and writes.

6.4.2.2 Transaction Manager

Just like a relational database transaction manager that provides a monotonically increasing write pointer (a pointer that gives write IDs for the database), a transaction manager assigns unique transaction IDs (a unique identifier for each transaction) for each transaction and maintains their states while transactions are in progress and committed. It also controls any invalid transaction states and conflicts with other running transactions in the same transaction boundaries. Basically, it manages the whole transaction process by controlling available transaction states. A transaction manager is simple and fast, keeps all required states in memory, and persists all states to a write-ahead log. You can configure transaction manager in high availability mode, one as active and other as standby, so that failover can be handled quickly.

Figure 6-2 shows a transaction with its read pointers, write pointers, and current state. When the client makes a call to start a transaction, the manager spawns a new transaction, increments its write pointer, and adds an entry into the transaction log. After the transaction is started and running, it increments its progress count and keeps all data in memory. Keeping transaction state in memory improves transaction performance.

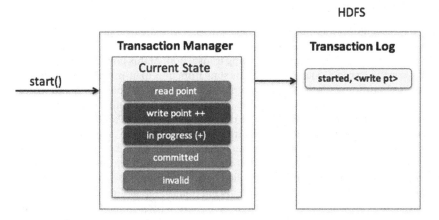

Figure 6-2. *Starting a transaction*

Figure 6-3 shows transaction's commit process. When the client has done its work, it makes a commit call to the manager to complete the transaction. If the transaction is successful, the in-progress pointer will be reduced by one, and the committed count will be increased by one. Finally, a log entry is added to record the transaction's successful completion.

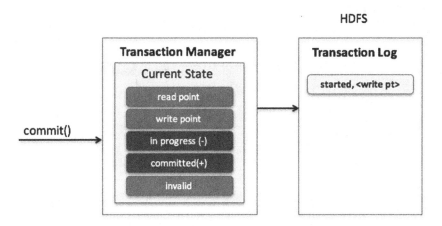

Figure 6-3. *Committing a transaction*

6.4.2.3   Transaction Processor Coprocessor

A transaction coprocessor is similar to the Phoenix coprocessor, which aggregates results or filters for reads on the HBase region server. Because a transaction keeps data versions or snapshots, the coprocessor is also used for cleaning up data from failed or invalid transactions.

6.4.3 Transaction Lifecycle

In HBase a transaction is started by a client like Phoenix with the help of a transaction manager (Phoenix uses Apache Tephra as transaction manager). The client places a RPC call to the transaction manager for starting transaction. At this point, transaction manager starts the transaction and changes its state from new to in-progress. The client then performs many operations (Put, Delete, etc.) and many other operations, and writes them to HBase. When all operations are done, the client tries to commit changes into HBase by invoking the commit RPC API. The transaction manager takes the changes and checks for any conflict with already running transactions. If there are no conflicts it saves changes into the database and associates a version to it. When the client tries committing changes and fails, an abort will be initiated. If aborting goes fine, the transaction will still be in a complete state and changes will be rolled back. If aborting fails, the transaction will lead to an invalid state and marked as an invalid transaction in the write log.

A transaction can also move to an invalid state if it is in progress and the transaction maximum time limit is exceeds. See Figure 6-4 for an illustration of the transaction lifecycle.

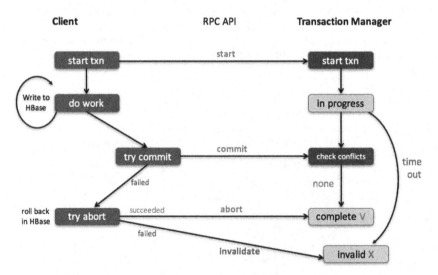

Figure 6-4. *Transaction Lifecycle*

6.4.4 Concurrency Control

When reading and writing happens at the same time, it is quite possible that the reader might see inconsistent data. For each transaction, HBase performs certain activities such as writes to Write-Ahead-Log(WAL), writes each data cell to memstore. It writes to WAL for disaster recovery and update an in-memory copy (memstore) of the data. These steps run in parallel for concurrent transactions and might lead to data inconsistency. There are many ways to solve this problem known as concurrency control methods. HBase uses underlying concurrency control methods to deal with concurrent transactions.

6.4.5   Multiversion Concurrency Control

Multiversion concurrency control(MVCC) is used to handle concurrent transactions. In this technique, each user sees a snapshot of database at an instant in time. Any changes made will not be seen by other users until the changes have been completed or committed. A newer version number is used to keep latest snapshot of the data for any data update. It keeps all versions of data and do not override old data.

HBase uses MVCC for read operations to avoid row locks. Mutiversion in HBase works as below for read and write operations.

Steps for read:

1.   A read timestamp is assigned for each read operation known as read point.

2.   Read point is highest integer for which all writes with write number less than or equal to that number have been completed.

3.   Data cell will be returned for a read of certain row, column combination with the matching row, column whose write number is the largest value that is less than or equal to the read point of read operation.

Steps for writes:

1.   A write number will be assigned for each write operation after acquiring row lock.

2.   Each data cell will store step one created write number in the write store.

3.   Write operation will be marked as completed by declaring its write number.

6.4.6   Optimistic Concurrency Control

Optimistic Concurrency Control(OCC) works on the basis that no other transaction interferes each other when they execute. This way they avoid cost of locking rows and tables. OCC verifies any data modifications by other transactions before committing and If the data is modified by other transaction, then just rollback all changes. This technique is good when there are rare conflicts like short transactions, disjoint partitioning of work etc.

6.5   Apache Tephra As a Transaction Manager

Apache Tephra is a transactional engine for distributed stores like HBase that provides support of multi-versioning and rollback. Tephra uses snapshot isolation for transactions. It uses HBase's native data versioning to provide multi-versioned concurrency control (MVCC) for transactional reads and writes. Multiversion concurrency control keeps a snapshot of data for each user, so each will be working with his or her own copy. Any changes made by the user will be visible until the final changes are complete, i.e. the transaction is committed. Tephra also enables optimistic control with the help of multi-version control and conflict detection.

Apache Tephra enables transaction capabilities in HBase across regions, tables, and remote procedure calls (RPCs). You can use your SQL knowledge for transactions, as Tephra has support for ACID properties.

6.6   Phoenix Transactions

Apache Phoenix provides full ACID support for cross row and cross table transactions for HBase, by using Apache Tephra as a transaction manager A powerful transaction manager with multi-versioned concurrency control and snapshot isolation for concurrent transactions.

By default, Phoenix does not enable transactions; you have to add enable transaction properties, for example by adding the phoenix.transactions.enabled property into the Hbase configuration file hbase-site.xml. The following properties are required in the HBase configuration file to work with Phoenix transactions.

```
<property>
  <name>phoenix.transactions.enabled</name>
  <value>true</value>
</property>
```

```
●●●                           ■ hbase-site.xml ﹀
/**
 * Licensed to the Apache Software Foundation (ASF) under one
 * or more contributor license agreements.  See the NOTICE file
 * distributed with this work for additional information
 * regarding copyright ownership.  The ASF licenses this file
 * to you under the Apache License, Version 2.0 (the
 * "License"); you may not use this file except in compliance
 * with the License.  You may obtain a copy of the License at
 *
 *     http://www.apache.org/licenses/LICENSE-2.0
 *
 * Unless required by applicable law or agreed to in writing, software
 * distributed under the License is distributed on an "AS IS" BASIS,
 * WITHOUT WARRANTIES OR CONDITIONS OF ANY KIND, either express or implied.
 * See the License for the specific language governing permissions and
 * limitations under the License.
 */|
-->
<configuration>
  <property>
    <name>hbase.regionserver.wal.codec</name>
    <value>org.apache.hadoop.hbase.regionserver.wal.IndexedWALEditCodec</value>
  </property>
  <property>
    <name>phoenix.transactions.enabled</name>
    <value>true</value>
  </property>

</configuration>
```

You need to add Apache Tephra configuration as a transaction manager into the server side `hbase-site.xml` and specify a snapshot directory in which to maintain Tephra snapshot versions. You must restart the region server after adding these configurations in order for them to take effect.

```
<property>
  <name>data.tx.snapshot.dir</name>
  <value>/tmp/tephra/snapshots</value>
</property>
```

After configuring the transaction manager, specify the transaction time limit for all transactions. It is important to set this time limit in order to handle any database transaction errors. Give this number as per your business SLAs and constraints. In general, do not open this window for a long time, because other threads might be waiting for the resources held by the failing transaction.

```
<property>
  <name>data.tx.timeout</name>
  <value>60</value>
</property>
```

When completed, your `hbase-site.xml` initialization file will contain all properties configured and should look like following Figure 6-5.

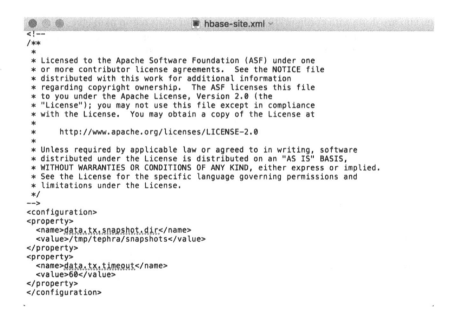

Figure 6-5. *hbase-site.xml with configuration properties*

```
● ● ●                          ■ hbase-site.xml ⌄
<?xml version="1.0"?>
<?xml-stylesheet type="text/xsl" href="configuration.xsl"?>
<!--
/**
 *
 * Licensed to the Apache Software Foundation (ASF) under one
 * or more contributor license agreements.  See the NOTICE file
 * distributed with this work for additional information
 * regarding copyright ownership.  The ASF licenses this file
 * to you under the Apache License, Version 2.0 (the
 * "License"); you may not use this file except in compliance
 * with the License.  You may obtain a copy of the License at
 *
 *     http://www.apache.org/licenses/LICENSE-2.0
 *
 * Unless required by applicable law or agreed to in writing, software
 * distributed under the License is distributed on an "AS IS" BASIS,
 * WITHOUT WARRANTIES OR CONDITIONS OF ANY KIND, either express or implied.
 * See the License for the specific language governing permissions and
 * limitations under the License.
 */
-->
<configuration>
<property>
  <name>phoenix.transactions.enabled</name>
  <value>true</value>
</property>
<property>
  <name>data.tx.snapshot.dir</name>
  <value>/tmp/tephra/snapshots</value>
</property>
<property>
  <name>data.tx.timeout</name>
  <value>60</value>
</property>
</configuration>
```

Figure 6-5. (*Continued*)

When you are done with configuration, then start your transaction manager (Apache Tephra) by executing the following command from Phoenix. You will find Tephra executable inside your Phoenix bin directory as shown in Figure 6-6.

```
shakils-MacBook-Pro:bin shakil$ pwd
/Users/shakil/tools/phoenix-4.8.0-HBase-1.2/bin
shakils-MacBook-Pro:bin shakil$ ls
config                               phoenix_utils.py
daemon.py                            phoenix_utils.pyc
end2endTest.py                       psql.py
hadoop-metrics2-hbase.properties     queryserver.py
hadoop-metrics2-phoenix.properties   readme.txt
hbase-site.xml                       sandbox-log4j.properties
log4j.properties                     sqlline-thin.py
performance.py                       sqlline.py
pherf-cluster.py                     tephra
pherf-standalone.py                  tephra-env.sh
phoenix_sandbox.py                   traceserver.py
```

Figure 6-6. *Tephra inside Phoenix bin*

```
./bin/tephra start
```

When starting, Phoenix will detect transactions and start functioning in transaction mode.

6.6.1   Enabling Transactions for Tables

You can specify transactional table either at the time of table creation or later updating table to support transactions.

While creating a table you must specify the 'TRANSACTIONAL=true' attribute in the table creation query.

Syntax:

```
CREATE TABLE table_name (column(s) data type(s)) TRANSACTIONAL=true;
```

For example, let's consider our supplier table example. We already saw how to create this table as non-transactional. Now we will create a transactional supplier table that will allow transactions.

```
CREATE TABLE SUPPLIER(SUPPLIER_ID BIGINT NOT NULL PRIMARY KEY,SUPPLIER_NAME
VARCHAR(30),CITY VARCHAR(40),STATE VARCHAR(30),ZIP INTEGER(10),COUNTRY
VARCHAR(100)) TRANSACTIONAL=true;
```

You can enable transactions for a table that has already been created as non-transactional by updating it to transactional.

Syntax:

```
ALTER TABLE table_name SET TRANSACTIONAL=true;
```

Let's enable our already-created table CUSTOMER to support transactions.

```
ALTER TABLE CUSTOMER SET  TRANSACTIONAL=true;
```

Now, operations performed on this table will be handled by Phoenix as transactional operations.

■ **Note**   If you enable transactions on a non-transactional table, it cannot be changed back to the non-transactional state.

6.6.2   Committing Transactions

When Phoenix is executing in transactional mode, then any statement we call in a query will initiate a new transaction. Until a COMMIT is executed, data will be in a raw state. When you have completed your changes, you can execute commit by simply entering the '!commit' command. This will complete your transaction, and all changes to the database will be visible to other users.

Let's see these steps by applying them to the ORDERS table. We will first query for all available orders, then execute some commands for updating and deleting orders.

```
SELECT * FROM ORDERS; -- Start a new transaction

UPSERT INTO ORDERS VALUES (10250,'2016-5-7', 108, 50,'A1100');

DELETE FROM ORDERS WHERE ORDER_ID='10248';

!commit  -- This will commit the transaction
```

on commit, everyone who looks at this table will see all changes.

6.7   Transaction Limitations in Phoenix

Phoenix is still maturing in transaction capabilities support at the time of writing. One of the limitations is manual cleanup of an invalid transactions list; a transaction that failed or became invalid due to a timeout is added to an invalid transactions list maintained by Tephra. An administrator is required to manually clear this list when there is a major compaction. This is limitation to Apache Tephra. Tephra developers are working on providing an automated cleanup for this list or a tool for administrators use to clear the list or a range of invalid transactions from the list.

Another limitation is to the number of snapshots for concurrent transactions when setting the version number property while creating a transactional table. This can result in the loss of some important log information.

While creating an asynchronous index to an existing transactional table, you should run a major compaction before issuing the CREATE INDEX ASYNC command; otherwise invalid and uncommitted transactions may appear in the index.

6.8   Summary

We discussed transactions in this chapter. Phoenix is used as a client for transaction enablement with the help of Apache Tephra (an Apache incubator project) transaction manager. Phoenix transactions support is still in beta phase till the writing of this book. This support will be improving as Tephra maturity grows. It is important to check Phoenix and HBase versions while doing transaction labs along with Tephra dependency requirement.

CHAPTER 7

■ ■ ■

Advanced Phoenix Concepts

It is important to consider data retrieval or search performance in achieving customer SLAs to get a business benefit out of it. We add indexes to improve data access time performance for relational as well as NoSQL databases. We will discuss in this chapter,how Phoenix indexing improves query performance for larger data sets. Along with Indexing, we will see how to work with phoenix user defined functions (UDF), writing custom UDFs and phoenix query server.

7.1   Secondary Indexes

For efficient access to data in a table, HBase creates and maintains a unique index on the row key and stores the data lexicographically. This allows applications to quickly retrieve data when primary key values are specified in a query. However, many applications might benefit from having one or more secondary indexes on columns in addition to the primary key, thus providing orthogonal access to data. This is definitely a huge challenge due to the ACID considerations in HBase.

Phoenix allows you to create multiple indexes on a table. While secondary index data structures add a lot of flexibility to the way data is modeled and efficiently queried, it adds a lot of complexity on the server end to keep the index in sync with the primary data. Phoenix uses custom coprocessors to sync data across indexes.

Secondary indexes can be created on data tables or on views. The index will be automatically kept in sync with the table as the data changes. For a given query, the Phoenix Query planner and optimizer chooses the best Query Plan. If, for example, the search query contains indexed columns, Phoenix internally rewrites the query to use the index table, rather than the data table, to fetch the data.

If a table has rows that are write-once and append-only, then the developer may set the table's IMMUTABLE_ROWS property to true, either up-front in the CREATE TABLE statement or afterward in an ALTER TABLE statement. This reduces the overhead at write time to maintain the index. If this property is not set on the table, then incremental index maintenance will be performed on the server side when the data changes.

There are two types of indexes that can be created in Phoenix: global indexes and local indexes.

© Shakil Akhtar and Ravi Magham 2017
S. Akhtar and R. Magham, *Pro Apache Phoenix*, DOI 10.1007/978-1-4842-2370-3_7

7.1.1   Global Index

Global indexes target read-heavy use cases. There is a minor performance hit during writes as the mutations (Put/Delete) have to be written to both the data table and to the indexes. HBase coprocessors provide hooks allowing them to be notified on various activities going on the WAL and the region server. These hooks help in constructing the necessary data that needs to be written to index tables. Scan queries perform better on global indexes as the framework rewrites queries to choose the optimal query plan and may decide to fetch data from index tables rather than from data tables. See Figure 7-1 for how global indexes look internally on the region server. As part of a query, the user can specify special hints to the query optimizer to choose one table over another. It's always a good practice to run the query through an Explain plan to better understand its implications.

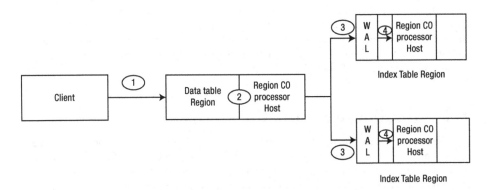

Figure 7-1. *Mutable Global Index*

Syntax:

```
CREATE INDEX  index_name
ON table (expression)
INCLUDE (column_refs)
[ASYNC]
[table_options] [SPLIT ON (constant)]
```

Example: Let's create an index on the CUSTOMER table that includes the state *column:*

```
0: jdbc:phoenix:localhost:2181> CREATE INDEX customer_state_indx ON customer (state);
6 rows affected (6.296 seconds)
```

0: jdbc:phoenix:localhost:2181> CREATE INDEX customer_state_indx ON customer (state);
6 rows affected (7.28 seconds)
0: jdbc:phoenix:localhost:2181>

Let's start an interactive HBase shell by starting a terminal and executing *'hbase shell'* and take a quick look at the index table.

```
$ hbase shell
```

```
$ scan 'CUSTOMER_STATE_INDX'
```

Apparently, for mutable indexes the row key format in the index table is in the format *{index_column} {primary_table_rowkey}*.

■ **Note** If the index_column is a variable length column, an empty byte separator is used to separate the fields. Here, the qualifier and the column family for the rows are the defaults, which are '0' and '_0'.

As stated above, Phoenix tries to sync the index table with the master table once the request for index creation is received. Since this is a synchronous process, you will have periods of time where the index table cannot be used for querying. To check the status of the index, execute the following command

```
0: jdbc:phoenix:localhost:2181> !tables CUSTOMER_STATE_INDX
```

This marks the INDEX_STATE as 'ACTIVE.' The other likely states that an index can have are BUILDING, USABLE, UNUSABLE, INACTIVE, DISABLE, and REBUILD.

Only when the index is in the 'ACTIVE' state will Phoenix use the index table, otherwise it uses the master table for queries.

■ **Note** If the master table is huge, you are likely to see a delay in the response from the "CREATE INDEX" query as Phoenix internally initiates an "UPSERT INTO .. SELECT" statement. Starting with Phoenix version 4.7, you can populate the index asynchronously by appending the "ASYNC" keyword.

To ensure consistency between the master data and index data, mutations received to the master table are synchronously sent to the index table. The way this is handled differs depending on whether the master table is mutable or immutable.

7.1.1.1   Immutable Tables

Implicitly, every HBase table is mutable. However, tables designed to store time series data, for example, do not update existing data as they are usually append-only, once-written. In such cases, you can mark the master table with an additional table option, "IMMUTABLE ROWS = true".

The primary contract of an immutable table is the fact that data, once written, doesn't change. If this contract is broken by the client, the framework cannot help much in resolving inconsistencies that arise.

Command to mark a table as immutable:

```
0: jdbc: phoenix:localhost:2181:/hbase> ALTER TABLE ORDERS SET IMMUTABLE_
ROWS = true;
```

```
0: jdbc: phoenix:localhost:2181> ALTER TABLE ORDERS SET IMMUTABLE_ROWS = true;
16/09/18 17:44:36 WARN query. ConnectionQueryServicesImpl: Attempt to cache
older version of ORDERS: current= 3, new=3
No rows affected (0.005 seconds)
```

Example: For the ORDER tables, the current *rowkey* is a concatenation of order_id and cust_id. To know the order amounts for each customer ID, the select query will turn to a full table scan:

```
0: jdbc: phoenix:localhost:2181:/hbase> EXPLAIN SELECT SUM(AMOUNT) FROM
ORDERS GROUP BY CUST_ID;
```

```
0: jdbc:phoenix:localhost:2181> explain select sum(amount) from ORDERS
group by cust_id;
+-----------------------------------------------------------+
|                           PLAN                            |
+-----------------------------------------------------------+
| CLIENT 1-CHUNK PARALLEL 1-WAY FULL SCAN OVER ORDERS       |
|     SERVER AGGREGATE INTO DISTINCT ROWS BY [CUST_ID]      |
| CLIENT MERGE SORT                                         |
+-----------------------------------------------------------+
```

Here, we observe the query performs a full table scan on the ORDERS table. Now, let's create a secondary index named 'customer_orders_indx' for which the row key is 'cust_id' and 'order_id'.

```
0: jdbc: phoenix:localhost:2181:/hbase> CREATE INDEX CUSTOMER_ORDER_INDX ON
ORDERS (CUST_ID, ORDER_ID) include (amount);
```

```
0: jdbc:phoenix:localhost:2181> CREATE INDEX CUSTOMER_ORDER_INDX ON
ORDERS(cust_id, order_id) include (amount);
5 rows affected (6.269 seconds)
0: jdbc:phoenix:localhost:2181>
```

Now, let's run the query

```
0: jdbc:phoenix:localhost:2181:/hbase> EXPLAIN SELECT SUM(AMOUNT) FROM
ORDERS GROUP BY CUST_ID;
```

```
0: jdbc:phoenix:localhost:2181> explain select sum(amount) from ORDERS
group by cust_id;
+------------------------------------------------------------------+
|                               PLAN                               |
+------------------------------------------------------------------+
| CLIENT 1-CHUNK PARALLEL 1-WAY FULL SCAN OVER CUSTOMER_ORDER_INDX |
|    SERVER AGGREGATE INTO ORDERED DISTINCT ROWS BY ["CUST_ID"]    |
+------------------------------------------------------------------+
2 rows selected (0.016 seconds)
0: jdbc:phoenix:localhost:2181>
```

Here, the same query does a full table scan on CUSTOMER_ORDER_INDX but performs better, as the row key starts with the **cust_id**. You can gain performance boost by skipping client side sorting for the query. This difference can be observed from the query execution plan by using EXPLAIN PLAN.

7.1.1.1.1   Consistency

For an immutable table, index maintenance is on the client side. By that, we mean that Phoenix internally creates mutations for the index table based on the input data in addition to the master table. The first write is to the master table, followed by writes to the index table. One important thing to note is the fact that there is a possibility of inconsistency in the index that can arise if the mutation to the master table is successful, but a failure arises while writing to the index tables. The client can keep retrying to ensure the upsert is successful. If the retries do not succeed, the master and index table will be out of sync.

Another fact to keep in mind is that we cannot prevent the data from being updated in a table merely by setting the table as IMMUTABLE, and if such an update happens, we will end up with inconsistent data.

7.1.1.2   Mutable Tables

For mutable tables, Phoenix works smartly by leveraging Region Observer Coprocessor hooks that behave like triggers in a database. With custom `RegionObservers` and WAL Observers, the framework intercepts the mutations (Put/Delete) to the master table, creates the necessary mutations for the index table and writes to it. From within the coprocessors, the writes are done in parallel on each of the index tables by running mutations for each table in a separate thread.

Index updates fail if any of the writes to the index table fail. When failures happen, Phoenix supports a choice of failure policies:

1. The failed index can be disabled so that it won't be used in queries, and automatic index rebuild begins from the point of failure. Once the rebuild succeeds, the index will be active.

2. Kill the region server policy: the region server tries to kill itself, thereby allowing it an opportunity to replay the WAL and repeat the process.

7.1.1.2.1   Configuration

Add the following property in the `hbase-site.xml` on the region servers.

```
<property>
  <name>hbase.regionserver.wal.codec</name>
  <value>
     org.apache.hadoop.hbase.regionserver.wal.IndexedWALEditCodec
  </value>
</property>
```

7.1.1.2.2   Consistency

Mutable indexes try to maintain consistency in the case of failures that occur during writes to index tables by having the region server die and retrying the operations during the replay of WAL. However, if the write to the data table failed, then the client has to retry the mutations to avoid inconsistent data.

7.1.2   Local Index

With global mutable and immutable indexes, the writes to an index table can often result in an update in multiple region servers. With local indexes, indexing is region wise. Until Phoenix version 4.8, Phoenix maintained an index table having same number of regions and boundaries as the data table, and there will be one-to-one mapping of data and index regions that are collocated on same region server.

The index data local to a data region is stored in a mapped index region. Local indexes provide an alternative where both the master and index tables are co-located in the same region. This gives a big boost to write-heavy workloads, as both the tables are co-located in the same region. Thus, it is recommended to use local indexes for cases of heavy writes, as it avoids the network overhead of sending index table updates to remote servers.

Until Phoenix version 4.8, the framework was piggy-backing on the custom load balancer and the region split/merge process through custom coprocessors to ensure both the master and local indexes regions were collocated. The rowkey of the local index tables was of the format

```
region_startkey + index_id + index_column_value + master_table_rowkey.
```

Local Indexes until Phoenix version 4.7 and its available components are shown in Figure 7-2.

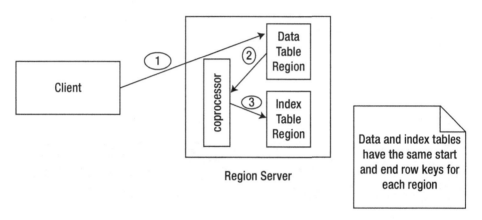

Figure 7-2. *Local Indexes until Phoenix 4.7*

Phoenix version 4.8 introduced many performance improvements for local indexes, as the local indexes are stored in separate column families in the same master table. We no longer have separate tables. Data for the index tables are in the column family 'L#0'. The rowkey of the local index in Phoenix version 4.8 is

```
region_startkey + index_id + index_column_value + master_table_rowkey
```

You can find changes in the formation of local Indexes and their intractions with region servers in Figure 7-3.

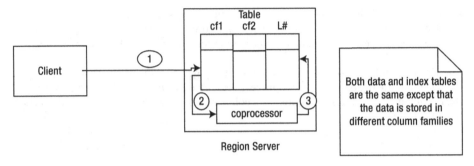

Figure 7-3. *Local Indexes in Phoenix 4.8*

Since we no longer have separate index tables, the meta-information of the index tables is stored in the SYSTEM.CATALOG table. Even though there was a separate table earlier, we store metadata in system.catalog table.

Let's get started by creating a local index on the ITEM table where we add a local index on 'supplier_id'.

Syntax:

```
0: jdbc:phoenix:localhost:2181:/hbase> CREATE LOCAL INDEX ITEM_SUPPLIER_
LINDX ON ITEM(supplier_id);
```

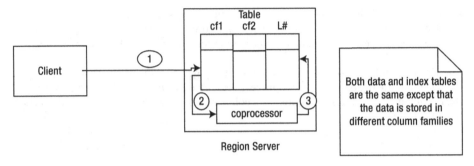

From the HBase shell, let's do a quick scan on the ITEM table. You will notice that we have a new column family, 'L#0', where L indicates a local index and 0 marks the default column family name. If we have a column in the include part of an index creation command with some column family, let's say 'cf1:c', then we will have one more column family, 'L#cf1', to store the key values of the first column 'c' local index on the table. The index number keeps increasing with the creation of local indexes on the table.

7.1.3 Covered Index

Apart from the fact that we can create secondary indexes with key columns, we can also include additional columns from the data table into the index. This helps in covering more queries where a query contains all the columns that can be fetched from the index, avoiding the costly call to the data table. This improves read performance to a large extent.

Syntax:

```
CREATE INDEX INDX_NAME ON TABLE_NAME (COL1, COL2...) INCLUDE (COLX, COLY);
```

Example:

```
CREATE INDEX CUSTOMER_ORDER_INDX ON ORDERS(CUST_ID, ORDER_ID) include (amount);
```

Here, we create an index which holds CUST_ID and ORDER_ID as key columns and 'amount' as a covered column in the table 'CUSTOMER_ORDER_INDX'.

Though data is stored redundantly in the master and the index tables, the performance gains covered indexes provide can easily offset the storage cost.

7.1.4 Functional Indexes

Functional indexes provide the ability to create indexes with expressions on one or more columns of a table. The expressions are evaluated on the incoming data table, and a corresponding UPSERT command is generated synchronously for the index table. By storing the evaluated expression at write time, we avoid the cost at fetch time. Queries that contain the expression will be redirected to the index table to fetch the information.

Example: Let's create a functional index with covered columns on a 'supplier' table

```
CREATE INDEX SUPPLIER_UPPER_NAME_INDX ON SUPPLIER (UPPER(SUPPLIER_NAME))
INCLUDE (STATE)
```

As we can observe, when the SELECT query contains the expression UPPER(SUPPLIER_NAME), the query is redirected to the index table rather than to the data table 'SUPPLIER'.

7.1.5 Index Consistency

Below is a quick outline of the consistency guarantees one can expect from the framework and the configurations that can help handle scenarios where the data and index tables are inconsistent.

1. If the table is a non-transactional immutable (where IMMUTABLE_ROWS= true is set as the table configuration) one, any failures that happen in the writes to data or index table need to be handled at the client end by doing a retry until success. An index is in an inconsistent state when the write to the data table went through fine but the write to index failed. On the other hand, if the write to data table itself failed, the index will remain in consistent state.

2. If the table is mutable non-transactional one and a failure is returned from a query, then the tables (data or index) can potentially be inconsistent. If the write to data table is success,

the index is one write behind. At this point, there are couple of configurations in hand that can be done to overcome the issue.

a) Allow writes to data table Is the default behavior where Phoenix allows writes to data table but disallows any to the index table. The index table is marked as 'DISABLED' Phoenix runs a background process to rebuild the index. No explicit configuration is required for this behavior. Once the index table is in sync with the data table, the state of the index table is changed back to 'ACTIVE'.

b) Disable further writes to data table till index is in sync with an automatic index rebuild. In this case, the index is still marked as 'ACTIVE' and is used for serving queries. Only that new writes aren't received till it is in sync with data table. phoenix.index.failure.block.write: blocks write to data table once a failure is noticed on index writes. Set to 'true' to enforce this. phoenix.index. failure.handling.rebuild: Phoenix does a rebuild of the index in the background by default. Since the default is 'true', no change is required.

c) Disable writes to index table with a manual rebuild. This is used in cases where the index is totally corrupt and requires a complete rebuild of the index. When a write to an index fail, Phoenix changes the state of the index to 'REBUILD'. phoenix.index.failure.handling. rebuild: Set this property to 'false' to disallow Phoenix to rebuild the index automatically. To excplicitly rebuild the index, execute the following command.

ALTER INDEX IF EXISTS INDX_TABLE ON DATA_TABLE REBUILD [ASYNC]

If you pass ASYNC, the index creation uses a Map Reduce job rather than rebuilding the index synchronously.

3. For local indexes, the data and local indexes can be in inconsistent state but phoenix tries to keep them in sync and it is quick because the local indexes are in the same Region Server. Starting 4.8, since local index are now in a different column family of the data table, the default HBase ACID property of consistency guarantees for a row will hold true there by ensuring we never have inconsistency.

4. Transaction tables are always in a consistent state.

7.2   User Defined Functions

Phoenix has a collection of built-in Functions (https://phoenix.apache.org/language/functions.html) as part of its standard library. Starting with Phoenix version 4.4.0, developers can write user-defined functions (UDFs) with custom code having application logic that processes column values during a query. Currently, developers can write scalar functions which take one input and return one output value. The UDFs can be used the same way as built-in functions in queries such as SELECT, UPSERT, DELETE, and Functional Indexes.

This feature provides many advantages for developers to write transformations in flexible ways that are outside the scope of the custom functions registry. A custom UDF has access to an entire row. The framework triggers a callback to your function as part of an HBase scan for each key value. The tuple passed to the evaluate method is the current state of the row.

7.2.1   Writing Custom User Defined Functions

Let's create a custom user defined function (UDF) "*hasVowels*" that checks if the input string contains a vowel. This simple example shows the power of custom user defined functions.

```java
import org.apache.hadoop.hbase.io.ImmutableBytesWritable;
import org.apache.phoenix.compile.KeyPart;
import org.apache.phoenix.expression.Expression
import org.apache.phoenix.expression.function.ScalarFuction;
import org.apache.phoenix.schema.tuple.Tuple;
import org.apache.phoenix.schema.types.PBoolean;
import org.apache.phoenix.schema.types.PDataType;
import org.apache.phoenix.schema.types.PVarchar;

import java.sql.SQLException;
import java.util.List;

/**
 *
 */
public class HasVowelsFunction extends ScalarFunction {

    private static final String FUNC_NAME = "hasVowels";

    @Override
    public PDataType getDataType() {
        return PBoolean.INSTANCE;
    }
```

```java
public HasVowelsFunction() {
}

public HasVowelsFunction(List<Expression> children) throws SQLException {
    super(children);
}

/**
 * Determines whether a function may be used to form
 * the start/stop key of a scan
 * @return the zero-based position of the argument to  traverse
 *  into to look for a primary key column reference, or
 *  {@value #NO_TRAVERSAL} if the function cannot be used to
 *  form the scan key.
 */
public int getKeyFormationTraversalIndex() {
    return NO_TRAVERSAL;
}

/**
 * Manufactures a KeyPart used to construct the KeyRange given
 * a constant and a comparison operator.
 * @param childPart the KeyPart formulated for the child expression
 * at the {@link #getKeyFormationTraversalIndex()} position.
 * @return the KeyPart for constructing the KeyRange for this function.
 */
public KeyPart newKeyPart(KeyPart childPart) {
    return null;
}

/**
 * Determines whether the result of the function invocation
 * will be ordered in the same way as the input to the function.
 * Returning YES enables an optimization to occur when a
 * GROUP BY contains function invocations using the leading PK
 * column(s).
 * @return YES if the function invocation will always preserve order for
 * the inputs versus the outputs and false otherwise, YES_IF_LAST if the
 * function preserves order, but any further column reference would not
 * continue to preserve order, and NO if the function does not preserve
 * order.
 */
public OrderPreserving preservesOrder() {
    return OrderPreserving.NO;
}

/**
 * is the method to be implemented which provides access to the Tuple
```

```java
     * @param tuple Single row result during scan iteration
     * @param ptr Pointer to byte value being accessed
     * @return
     */
    @Override
    public boolean evaluate(Tuple tuple, ImmutableBytesWritable ptr) {
        Expression child = children.get(0);
        if (!child.evaluate(tuple, ptr)) {
            return false;
        }

        String inputStr = (String) PVarchar.INSTANCE.toObject(ptr, child.
          getSortOrder());
        if (inputStr == null) {
            return true;
        }

        boolean vowelFound = false;
        for(char each : inputStr.toCharArray()) {
            if(vowelFound) {
                break;
            }
            switch(each) {
                case 'a':
                case 'e':
                case 'i':
                case 'o':
                case 'u':
                    ptr.set(PBoolean.INSTANCE.toBytes(true));
                    vowelFound = true;
                    break;
                default:
            }
        }
        if(!vowelFound) {
            ptr.set(PBoolean.INSTANCE.toBytes(false));
        }

        return true;
    }
    @Override
    public String getName() {
        return FUNC_NAME;
    }
}
```

7.2.1.1   Configuration

Registering custom functions requires minor configuration changes as shown in Table 7-1 needs to be set in hbase-site.xml. See Table 7-1 for properties and their corresponding values.

Table 7-1. *UDF Configuration Properties*

Property name	Value
phoenix.functions.allowUserDefinedFunctions	true
hbase.dynamic.jars.dir	${hbase.rootdir}/lib
hbase.local.dir	${hbase.tmp.dir}/local/

7.2.1.2   Runtime Environment

To register the function with Phoenix, first copy the compiled artifact into a JAR and place it in any directory on HDFS. By default, Phoenix copies the UDFs artifacts into the "*$hbase.local.dir*".

```
$ hadoop fs -copyFromLocal udfs.jar /hbase/lib/
```

Next, register the custom function with Phoenix.
Syntax:

```
CREATE [TEMPORARY] FUNCTION {function_name}
RETURN {phoenix_data_type}  as {class_name}    USING JAR {hdfs_jar_path}
```

Example:

```
0: jdbc:phoenix:localhost:2181:/hbase> CREATE FUNCTION hasVowels(varchar)
returns BOOLEAN as 'HasVowelsFunction'  USING JAR  '/hbase/lib/udfs.jar';
```

Apparently, when we register a custom UDF function, Phoenix stores the metadata, including the UDF JAR location, function name, return type, and the number of arguments to the function, in a table named 'SYSTEM.FUNCTION'.

A couple of limitations that often arise with UDFs are:

1. Since the JARs are loaded on the HBase RegionServer, any minor changes to UDFs would mean creating a new JAR and adding that to the HBase dynamic lib directory. If your server goes down, then you can redeploy the function.

2. While executing a query with a UDF, the dynamic class loader copies the artifact containing the function to {hbase.local.dir}/jars at the Phoenix client. The JARs must be deleted manually once a function is deleted.

3. Currently, only scalar functions are supported. You cannot register custom aggregate functions.

7.3   Phoenix Query Server

By default, clients can connect to Phoenix-backed HBase through the JDBC driver. This presents a couple of challenges when integrating from non-JVM based client languages. Also, the query plan, query execution, and results processing on the client can impact the client process. The JDBC driver primarily acts as a thick client. Figure 7-4 describes how the Phoenix query server interacts with HBase region servers.

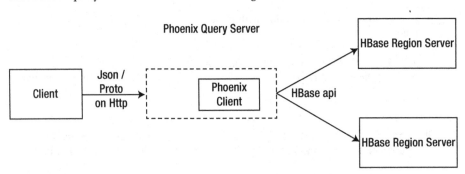

Figure 7-4. *Phoenix Query Server*

Phoenix Query Server (PQS) complements this by allowing the clients use a thin driver and allowing the query plan, execution, and processing on an external server process to be scaled horizontally independent of the client process, as the query server is stateless. The thin driver is based on the Avatica (https://calcite.apache.org/avatica/) framework, which provides an API between the client and the server. In Avatica, the server is an HTTP server and the client is a simple JDBC driver that allows the client to communicate over protocol buffers or JSON. Wire protocols provide the flexibility to have clients in non-JVM languages.

7.3.1   Download

Phoenix provides thin driver artifacts used by the client process and server artifacts to start the Phoenix Query server as part of the tar download.

7.3.2   Installation

A typical installation runs the query server on the hosts that run the HBase region servers. Though it doesn't need to be a one-to-one mapping to the region server count, it is preferred to run one instance of the server on one host.

7.3.3   Setup

Export the following environment variables with the exact values based on your environment in either ~/.ssh/bash_profile or ~/.ssh/.bashrc.

```
export HBASE_CONF_DIR=<path_to_hbase_conf>
export PHOENIX_LIB_DIR=<path_to_phoenix_lib_directory>
export HADOOP_CONF_DIR=<path_to_hadoop_conf>
```

7.3.4   Starting PQS

Navigate to the base Phoenix directory and start the query server. The basic usage is:

```
$ bin/queryserver.py [start|stop|makeWinServiceDesc]  [-Dhadoop=configs]
```

To start the service in the background, run the following command.

```
$ bin/queryserver.py start background
```

The logs of the query server are written to the same HBase logs directory with the default file name format <username>-queryserver.log.

The query server internally starts a Jetty HTTP server on port 8765. To change the port number, set a property 'phoenix.queryserver.http.port' in hbase-site.xml.

The default wire API for serializing the communication between client and server uses protocol buffers. To change this, set the property 'phoenix.queryserver. serialization' to 'json'.

7.3.5   Client

Until now the driver protocol had the syntax "jdbc:phoenix:<zk host>:<zk port>". However, to use the thin client, the syntax of the protocol URL to be constructed is in the format "jdbc:phoenix:thin:url=<scheme>://<server-hostname>:<port>". The following table shows template parameters and their descriptions. You can replace values in value column in Table 7-2 with your environment values.

Table 7-2. Phoenix Query Server configuration properties

Property	Value
scheme	http
server-host-name	The hostname of the server
port	The http port of the query server

7.3.6   Usage

For a quick start, you can use the `sqline-thin.py` script to start communicating to the query service. Let's start by connecting to a local query server.

Ex. `$ bin/sqlline-thin.py <http_query_server_url> <sql_file>`

Let's create a simple file 'employee_ddl.sql' with the following DDL query to create the employee table.

```
CREATE TABLE IF NOT EXISTS EMPLOYEE (
        EMP_ID INTEGER NOT NULL,
        EMP_NAME VARCHAR ,
        CONTACT VARCHAR ,
        HIRE_DATE DATE,
        SALARY INTEGER
CONSTRAINT PK PRIMARY KEY (EMP_ID));
```

Let's run the table creation through the query server.

```
$ bin/sqlline-thin.py http://localhost:8765 employee_ddl.sql
```

```
Connected to: Apache Phoenix (version unknown version)
Driver: Phoenix Remote JDBC Driver (version unknown version)
Autocommit status: true
Transaction isolation: TRANSACTION_READ_COMMITTED
Building list of tables and columns for tab-completion (set fastconnect to true to skip)...
128/128 (100%) Done
Done
1/1       CREATE TABLE IF NOT EXISTS EMPLOYEE (
EMP_ID INTEGER NOT NULL,
EMP_NAME VARCHAR ,
CONTACT VARCHAR ,
HIRE_DATE DATE,
SALARY INTEGER
CONSTRAINT PK PRIMARY KEY (EMP_ID));
No rows affected (2.341 seconds)
Closing: org.apache.calcite.avatica.AvaticaJdbc41Factory$AvaticaJdbc41Connection
sqlline version 1.1.9
```

After the successful completion, let's view the employee table schema.

```
$ /bin/sqlline-thin.py http://localhost:8765
```

7.3.7   Additional PQS Features

The Phoenix Query Server (PQS) supports connecting to a secure HBase cluster.

Since PQS is inherently wrapped as an HTTP server, it's easy to have it running behind load balancers to achieve better availability.

7.3.7.1   Gotchas

Ordering of results from server can be a problem. Apparently the query server collects data from the backend region servers and streams them across to the client. Unless the property 'phoenix.query.force.rowkeyorder' is specified in the hbase-site.xml, the ordering of the results returned can vary for each call for the same query.

Backwards compatibility isn't guaranteed on the JSON transport API. However, with protocol buffers, backwards compatibility can be better achieved moving forward.

7.4   Summary

In this chapter we described advanced concepts including user-defined functions, indexing, and the Phoenix query server. User-defined functions can be customized to a greater extent to make it more flexible for business use cases. We saw how to deal with the Phoenix query server, its installation, and other constructs. In later chapters we will see how to integrate Phoenix with other available technologies.

CHAPTER 8

■ ■ ■

Integrating Phoenix with Other Frameworks

In previous chapters we discussed Phoenix fundamental constructs, querying using Phoenix and other advanced concepts. We can also use Phoenix with other existing technologies in the Hadoop ecosystem. This chapter focuses on Phoenix integration with Spark, Pig, Hive, and MapReduce frameworks. Phoenix is a powerful yet easy to use framework for integrating with Spark for real time data analysis and massively parallel MapReduce jobs. It can also act as a catalyst for Hive and Pig-like scripting to achieve better performance in big data analytics space. We will discuss all these integration points available in Phoenix and how to use them effectively for massive data sets.

8.1   Hadoop Ecosystem

Apache Phoenix plays very well with the other frameworks like Apache Spark, Apache Pig, and Apache Hive in the Hadoop ecosystem, all of which provide handlers to read and write from HBase. Though we can use these frameworks to directly read and write to Phoenix, you get better query performance using the respective handlers provided by Phoenix, as they transform data types from the native format to the external framework data types.

8.2   MapReduce Integration

MapReduce is a programming paradigm for performing processing on large datasets at a massive scale on commodity hardware in a reliable and fault tolerant manner. It brought about a mind shift of doing data processing on large datasets by moving the computation to the data rather than the other way round. Efficient scheduler algorithms help improve performance of MapReduce jobs by taking advantage of data locality in addition to monitoring and rerunning failed jobs.

The workings of a MapReduce job are very simple as it starts off with processing small splits of the input dataset by mapping tasks in parallel. The framework then sorts the mapper output, which is subsequently fetched by the reduce tasks. The reduce tasks do the final aggregation on each group per key in the reduce function.

© Shakil Akhtar and Ravi Magham 2017
S. Akhtar and R. Magham, *Pro Apache Phoenix*, DOI 10.1007/978-1-4842-2370-3_8

Though Phoenix supports SELECT and UPSERT statements at scale using the underlying HBase API, quite often when we need to perform large data processing tasks such as index building, aggregations on large tables, leveraging the driver API can become a bottleneck as the client can consume a lot of memory, affecting the performance of the application. To support use cases where batch processing is acceptable, we can write MapReduce jobs that can read or write to Phoenix tables.

Phoenix leverages the DBInputFormat (https://hadoop.apache.org/docs/ r2.7.2/api/org/apache/hadoop/mapreduce/lib/db/DBInputFormat.html) and DBOutputFormat (https://hadoop.apache.org/docs/r2.7.2/api/org/apache/ hadoop/mapreduce/lib/db/DBOutputFormat.html) APIs for reading and writing in MapReduce jobs. Users can provide the exact SELECT query or pass in the list of columns that they would like to read from Phoenix, and the underlying library marshalls the underlying byte streams to the custom Writable class.

The custom InputFormat class PhoenixInputFormat internally computes the query plan and optimizes on the number of input splits based on the input query. The PhoenixOutputFormat serializes the Java data types onto byte streams before writing to HBase.

8.2.1   Setup

Include the phoenix-client-<phoenix_version>.jar in the classpath of the uber MapReduce job, thereby ensuring the driver program has access to tables, and compute the query plan.

Example:

Let's write a MapReduce program that reads from **ORDERS** table and compute the total amount per customer id and write the result back to the "**ORDER_STATS**" table.

```
package com.apress.phoenix.mapreduce;

import org.apache.hadoop.conf.Configuration;
import org.apache.hadoop.conf.Configured;
import org.apache.hadoop.hbase.HBaseConfiguration;
import org.apache.hadoop.hbase.mapreduce.TableMapReduceUtil;
import org.apache.hadoop.io.DoubleWritable;
import org.apache.hadoop.io.LongWritable;
import org.apache.hadoop.io.NullWritable;
import org.apache.hadoop.io.Writable;
import org.apache.hadoop.mapreduce.Job;
import org.apache.hadoop.mapreduce.Mapper;
import org.apache.hadoop.mapreduce.Reducer;
import org.apache.hadoop.mapreduce.lib.db.DBWritable;
import org.apache.hadoop.util.Tool;
import org.apache.phoenix.mapreduce.PhoenixOutputFormat;
import org.apache.phoenix.mapreduce.util.PhoenixMapReduceUtil;

import org.slf4j.Logger;
import org.slf4j.LoggerFactory;
```

```java
import java.io.DataInput;
import java.io.DataOutput;
import java.io.IOException;
import java.sql.PreparedStatement;
import java.sql.ResultSet;
import java.sql.SQLException;

/**
*
*/
public class OrderStatsApp extends Configured implements Tool {

    private static final Logger LOG = LoggerFactory.getLogger(OrderStatsApp.class);

    public int run(String[] args) throws Exception {
        try {
            final Configuration configuration = HBaseConfiguration.create(getConf());
            setConf(configuration);
            final Job job = Job.getInstance(configuration, "phoenix-mr-order_
                                                           stats-job");
            final String selectQuery = "SELECT ORDER_ID, CUST_ID, AMOUNT FROM
                                ORDERS ";

            // set the input table and select query. you can also pass in the
               list of columns
            PhoenixMapReduceUtil.setInput(job, OrderWritable.class, "ORDERS",
               selectQuery);
            // set the output table name and the list of columns.
            PhoenixMapReduceUtil.setOutput(job, "ORDER_STATS", "CUST_ID, AMOUNT");

            job.setMapperClass(OrderMapper.class);
            job.setReducerClass(OrderReducer.class);
            job.setOutputFormatClass(PhoenixOutputFormat.class);

            job.setMapOutputKeyClass(LongWritable.class);
            job.setMapOutputValueClass(DoubleWritable.class);
            job.setOutputKeyClass(NullWritable.class);
            job.setOutputValueClass(OrderWritable.class);
            TableMapReduceUtil.addDependencyJars(job);
            job.waitForCompletion(true);
            return 0;
        } catch (Exception ex) {
            LOG.error(String.format("An exception [%s] occurred while
                performing the job: ", ex.getMessage()));
            return -1;
        }
    }
}
```

```java
public static void main(String[] args) throws Exception{
    int status =ToolRunner.run( new OrderStatsApp(), args);
    System.exit(status);
}

public static class OrderMapper extends Mapper<NullWritable,
OrderWritable, LongWritable, DoubleWritable> {

    private LongWritable customerId = new LongWritable();
    private DoubleWritable amount = new DoubleWritable();

    @Override
    protected void map(NullWritable key, OrderWritable order,
        Context context) throws IOException, InterruptedException {
        // leaving out data validation for brevity.
        customerId.set(order.customerId);
        amount.set(order.amount);
        context.write(customerId, amount);
    }
}

public static class OrderReducer extends Reducer<LongWritable,
    DoubleWritable, NullWritable, OrderWritable> {

    @Override
    protected void reduce(LongWritable key, Iterable<DoubleWritable>
    amounts, Context context) throws IOException, InterruptedException {
        // keeping only the core logic here.
        double totalValue = 0.0;
        for(DoubleWritable amount : amounts) {
            totalValue += amount.get();
        }

        context.write(NullWritable.get(), new OrderWritable(key.get(),
            totalValue));
    }
}

public static class OrderWritable implements DBWritable, Writable {

    private Long customerId;
    private Double amount;

    public OrderWritable() {

    }
```

```java
    public OrderWritable(Long customerId, Double amount) {
        this.customerId = customerId;
        this.amount = amount;
    }
    public void write(PreparedStatement preparedStatement) throws SQLException {
        preparedStatement.setLong(1, customerId);
        preparedStatement.setDouble(2, amount);
    }

    public void readFields(ResultSet resultSet) throws SQLException {
        customerId = resultSet.getLong("CUST_ID");
        amount = resultSet.getDouble("AMOUNT");
    }

    public void write(DataOutput dataOutput) throws IOException {
        dataOutput.writeLong(customerId);
        dataOutput.writeDouble(amount);
    }

    public void readFields(DataInput dataInput) throws IOException {
        this.customerId = dataInput.readLong();
        this.amount = dataInput.readDouble();
    }
  }
}
```

From the above program we can see how easy it is to write a MapReduce job to process data at scale.

Gotchas:

a. Group By and Distinct clause queries aren't supported as part of input query.

b. We can apply functions on columns by passing in the explicit SELECT query.

In the previous chapters we have seen that, by default, index creation is a synchronous process, and it can be a challenge to scale it up if the data (master) table is large and we created an index. Starting with Phoenix 4.5, there is support for building the index asynchronously using a MapReduce job.

8.3   Apache Spark Integration

Apache Spark is an open source processing engine built for large scale processing of data. Its ease of programming allows for rapid development of data pipelines for both bounded and unbounded streams. It is being widely adopted in data engineering and developing iterative machine learning models.

Apart from the diverse data sources that Spark can access, there is native support for reading and writing to Phoenix using the Spark API. Users interested in the RDD approach to development can use PhoenixRDD, while others can use Dataframe, which operates on creating relational transformations.

8.3.1 Setup

Copy the artifact phoenix-spark-<phoenix_version>-Hbase-<hbase_version>.jar from the downloaded distribution and copy it to a location, say /usr/local/spark.

As part of spark-submit.sh to run a spark job, add the following configuration parameter.

--jars /usr/local/spark/phoenix-spark-<phoenix_version>.jar

Example: Reading and Writing to Phoenix using RDD

Below is a sample Spark program to read from the 'ORDERS' table and compute the total amount by customer ID.

```scala
package com.apress.phoenix.spark

import org.apache.spark.SparkConf
import org.apache.spark.rdd.RDD

/**
 *
 */
object PhoenixSparkRDDApp {

  def main(args: Array[String]) {

    import org.apache.spark.SparkContext
    import org.apache.phoenix.spark._

    val zkQuorum = "localhost:2181"
    val master = "local[*]"
    val sparkConf = new SparkConf()
    sparkConf.setAppName("phoenix-spark-save")
      .setMaster(s"${master}")

    val sc = new SparkContext(sparkConf)

    // read from orders phoenix table
    val rdd: RDD[Map[String, AnyRef]] = sc.phoenixTableAsRDD("ORDERS", Seq.
    apply("ORDER_ID", "CUST_ID", "AMOUNT"),
      zkUrl = Some.apply(s"${zkQuorum}")
    )
```

```scala
    val result = rdd.map(row => (row("CUST_ID").asInstanceOf[Long],
(row("AMOUNT").asInstanceOf[java.math.BigDecimal]).doubleValue()))
        .reduceByKey(_ + _)

    // save to customer_stats phoenix table.
    result.saveToPhoenix(
            "CUSTOMER_STATS", Seq("CUST_ID","AMOUNT"), zkUrl = Some.apply(s"
${zkQuorum}"))

    }
}
```

8.3.2   Reading and Writing Using Dataframe

```scala
package com.apress.phoenix.spark

import org.apache.spark.SparkConf
import org.apache.spark.rdd.RDD
import org.apache.spark.sql.SQLContext

/**
 *
 */
object PhoenixSparkDfApp {

  def main(args: Array[String]) {

    import org.apache.spark.SparkContext
    import org.apache.phoenix.spark._

    val zkQuorum = "localhost:2181"
    val master = "local[*]"
    val sparkConf = new SparkConf()
    sparkConf.setAppName("phoenix-spark-save")
      .setMaster(s"${master}")

    val sc = new SparkContext(sparkConf)
    val sqlContext = new SQLContext(sc)

    // read from orders phoenix table
    val df = sqlContext.phoenixTableAsDataFrame("ORDERS", Seq.apply
    ("ORDER_ID", "CUST_ID", "QUANTITY"),
            zkUrl = Some.apply(s"${zkQuorum}")
    )
```

```
val result = df.rdd.map(row => (row.getLong(1), row.getLong(2))).
            reduceByKey(_ + _)
// save to customer_stats phoenix table.
result.saveToPhoenix("CUSTOMER_STATS", Seq("CUST_ID", "QUANTITY"), zkUrl =
Some.apply(s"${zkQuorum}"))

  }
}
```

Gotchas:

- The Spark plugin doesn't support bulk loading of data into Phoenix tables.

- For Java users, going through the route of Dataframe is simpler than RDD as the PhoenixRDD cannot be invoked from Java.

8.4 Apache Hive Integration

Apache Hive is a data warehouse system on Hadoop. To make data access easier for non-programmers, it provides a simpler SQL-like language called HiveQL. Hive queries can be converted to MapReduce, Spark, or Tez jobs transparently. By abstracting the underlying storage and providing a simpler query language, Hive allows users to easily manipulate and perform various transformations using the various built-in and custom user defined functions (UDFs).

Starting with Phoenix version 4.8.0, users can use the custom PhoenixHiveHandler to read data from Phoenix in Hive.

8.4.1 Setup

Have the jar phoenix-<phoenix_version>-Hbase-<hbase_version>-hive.jar in the Hive classpath. From the Hive shell, execute the following command

```
ADD JAR /path-to/phoenix-<phoenix_version>-Hbase-<hbase_version>-hive.jar
```

Though the path to the JAR can be a URI referring to the local system, storing it on a distributed file system like HDFS or S3 is preferred, as all the nodes in the cluster have access to the path. Additionally, you can update the auxiliary path configuration parameter hive.aux.jars.path (https://cwiki.apache.org/confluence/display/Hive/AdminManual+Configuration), specifying the URI to the JAR in hive-site.xml or as part of the Hive client.

Example:

```
$ bin/hive  --auxpath= /path-to/phoenix-<phoenix_version>-Hbase-<hbase_
version>-hive.jar
```

In ${HIVE_HOME}/conf/hive-site.xml

```
<property>
        <name>hive.aux.jars.path</name>
        <value>/path-to/phoenix-<phoenix_version>-Hbase-<hbase_version>-hive.
        jar</value>
    </property>
```

8.4.2 Table Creation

Hive tables can be either EXTERNAL or INTERNAL; the difference primarily lies in who is managing the lifecycle of the table and its data. For INTERNAL tables, both data and lifecycle are managed by Hive; for EXTERNAL tables, only the metadata is managed by Hive.

```
CREATE [EXTERNAL] TABLE ORDERS
(
    id int,
    custid int,
    order_date date,
    amount double,
    quantity int
)
STORED BY 'org.apache.phoenix.hive.PhoenixStorageHandler'

TBLPROPERTIES (
        "phoenix.table.name" = "orders",
        "phoenix.zookeeper.quorum" = "zk_quorum",
        "phoenix.rowkeys" = "id, custid",
        "phoenix.column.mapping" = "id:order_id, custid:cust_id,
                order_date:order_date, amount:amount, quantity:quantity",
        "phoenix.table.options"   = "SALT_BUCKETS=10"
);
```

■ **Note** The property "phoenix.column.mapping" maps each column in Hive with Phoenix. The mapping is a ',' separated map of <hive_column> : <phoenix_column>.

Any additional properties that need to be passed to Phoenix tables can be passed as part of TBLPROPERTIES.

Executing the above command creates a table entry in the Hive metastore and also creates a Phoenix table.

8.5 Apache Pig Integration

Apache Pig is a high level language to process and store data on Hadoop. Through PigLatin scripts, we can define high level analyses of data processing as data flows, rather than explicitly writing native MapReduce jobs. The scripts are transformed into a series of MapReduce jobs to be run on the Hadoop cluster.

Users can use the PhoenixHBaseLoader and PhoenixHBaseStorage to load and store data to tables backed by Phoenix.

8.5.1 Setup

To either load or store data to Phoenix from Pig, we need to register the phoenix-pig-<phoenix_version>-HBase-<hbase_version>.jar in the pig script using the REGISTER (https://pig.apache.org/docs/r0.16.0/basic.html#register-jar) command.

```
REGISTER /path/to/phoenix-pig.jar
```

We can also pass the JAR path as part of configuration parameter 'pig.additional.jars.uris' as

```
$pig -Dpig.additional.jars.uris=/path/to/phoenix-pig.jar script.pig
```

8.5.2 Accessing Data from Phoenix

When accessing data from tables backed by Phoenix, we can specify either the table name followed by the list of columns or an SQL query.

```
REGISTER hdfs://apps/pig/lib/phoenix-pig.jar
ORDER = LOAD 'hbase://table/ORDERS' using    org.apache.phoenix.pig.
PhoenixHBaseLoader('zookeeper_quorum_uri');

REGISTER hdfs://apps/pig/lib/phoenix-pig.jar
ORDER = LOAD 'hbase://table/ORDERS/ORDER_ID, CUST_ID' using    org.apache.
phoenix.pig.PhoenixHBaseLoader('zookeeper_quorum_uri');

REGISTER hdfs://apps/pig/lib/phoenix-pig.jar
ORDER = LOAD 'hbase://query/SELECT ORDER_ID, CUST_ID FROM ORDERS' using
org.apache.phoenix.pig.PhoenixHBaseLoader('zookeeper_quorum_uri');
```

Internally, the PhoenixHBaseLoader converts the LOAD definition to a SELECT query which fetches data from multiple regions of the table.

8.5.3 Storing Data to Phoenix

PhoenixHBaseStorage allows storing into Phoenix tables. It internally maps the Pig data types to Phoenix data types and serializes them correctly.

```
REGISTER hdfs://apps/pig/lib/phoenix-pig.jar
A = LOAD '/path/to/data' USING PigStorage('\t') as (a:chararray,
b:chararray, c: datetime);
```

```
STORE A into 'hbase://phoenix-table' using
    org.apache.phoenix.pig.PhoenixHBaseStorage('${zookeeper.quorum}',
    '-batchSize 100');
```

```
// the second argument to PhoenixHBaseStorage is batch commit interval.
```

In both cases, Phoenix takes care of the necessary mapping between Pig schema and Phoenix data types.

Gotchas:

We cannot use AGGREGATE, GROUP BY, LIMIT, or DISTINCT keywords in the query part of the LOAD function.

8.6 Apache Flume Integration

Flume is a distributed, reliable log aggregation service to continuously stream data from sources onto sinks which can be HDFS or HBase. Its support for contextual routing and ease of extending and customization makes it a great tool for draining events to multiple sinks. In a typical installation, Flume agents run alongside the cluster with a configuration of the source which allows the ability to poll or pull data to multiplex or pass on to channels. Channels work as buffered queues thus avoiding data volume spikes.

Events in channels are persisted till sinks explicitly remove them as parts of transactions after writing them to the destination locations. Sinks are pluggable, and Phoenix provides custom sinks, leveraging the pluggability behavior.

8.6.1 Setup

The Phoenix Flume plugin needs to be registered with Flume. Copy the JAR phoenix-flume-<phoenix_version>-HBase-<hbase_version>.jar and place it in the $FLUME_HOME/plugins.d/phoenix-sink/lib directory.

8.6.2 Configuration

Let's configure a single source and a sink for Phoenix by creating a simple configuration file named phoenix-agent.conf. Here, we will stream data from Kafka to Phoenix.

```
# main components
agent.sources=kcollector
agent.sinks=phoenix-sink
agent.channels=memoryChannel
```

```
#configuring source
agent.sources.kcollector.type = org.apache.flume.source.kafka.KafkaSource
agent.sources.kcollector.channels = memoryChannel
```

```
agent.sources.kcollector.zookeeperConnect = localhost:2181
agent.sources.kcollector.topic = test
agent.sources.kcollector.groupId = flume_to_phoenix
agent.sources.kcollector.kafka.consumer.timeout.ms = 100

#configure channel
agent.channels.memoryChannel.type=memory
agent.channels.memoryChannel.byteCapacityBufferPercentage=20
agent.channels.memoryChannel.transactionCapacity=100

#configure sink
agent.sinks.phoenix-sink.type=org.apache.phoenix.flume.sink.PhoenixSink
agent.sinks.phoenix-sink.channel=memoryChannel
agent.sinks.phoenix-sink.batchSize=100
agent.sinks.phoenix-sink.table=TEST
agent.sinks.phoenix-sink.ddl=CREATE TABLE IF NOT EXISTS TEST(uid VARCHAT NOT
NULL, msg VARCHAR CONSTRAINT pk PRIMARY KEY(uid))
agent.sinks.phoenix-sink.zookeeperQuorum=localhost
agent.sinks.phoenix-sink.serializer=REGEX
agent.sinks.phoenix-sink.serializer.rowkeyType=uuid
agent.sinks.phoenix-sink.serializer.regex=([^]*)
agent.sinks.phoenix-sink.serializer.columns=msg
```

8.6.3   Running the Above Setup

Open a terminal and run the following command.

```
$ bin/flume-ng agent -f conf/phoenix-agent.conf -c ./conf -n agent
```

In the above setup, we take in each message from Kafka, convert it into a String, and write to Phoenix.

8.7   Summary

It is important for any technology to provide integration points and custom behavior that can be customized as per user need. We saw how good phoenix deals with these philosophies and exposes many integration points to extend the framework to the next level. Although Hadoop is much popular and we might have used hive or pig for our projects, but we always look for better ways to work on data analysis for greater system performance. You should consider phoenix as a new participant in our existing system portfolio. Phoenix hides complexities and lets you work with older systems using hive, pig etc. with phoenix integration points extensions. This chapter brings important information for those who deal with the polyglot of databases and consume large data from data lake.

## CHAPTER 9

Tools & Tuning

We have seen how phoenix can help us for big data analysis by writing simple easy to use queries and other features for handling HBase storage data in an efficient way. The important thing for any database query engine is its performance and how this can support increasing load with optimal performance. Phoenix provides many configurations and suggests many ways by which we can meet our performance SLAs. This chapter is all about performance and available phoenix tools to understand phoenix internal tuning, debugging, and handling any such related issues in our production environment.

9.1   Phoenix Tracing Server

Most internet services that are built on complex distributed systems fan out a single request to multiple backend system calls to process the request and respond. Often it becomes necessary to understand any performance bottlenecks in a deeply nested set of backend services to help aid in performance optimizations and root cause analysis.

To enable users to better understand and monitor performance and latency that arise at either the client or server end, Phoenix integrates with Apache HTrace (`http://htrace.incubator.apache.org`). HTrace is a tracing library that provides traces across network boundaries on a sampled subset of requests that span distributed systems like the Hadoop Distributed File System (HDFS) and HBase. By leveraging the HTrace library, Phoenix sends these traces from the client and server to a Phoenix table. It extends further by providing a web server to view these traces, thereby providing a unique opportunity for developers and the operations team in having a 360 degree view of the request/response workflow.

Though this chapter will not be a deep dive into HTrace, we will give an overview with enough depth to provide a better understanding of how Phoenix and Htrace work together to address performance issues.

9.1.1   Trace

Each user initiated request is termed a TraceScope. Trace manages the lifecycle of spans.

9.1.2 Span

Each trace can be made up of multiple spans where each span, identified by a pseudo-random number, is mapped to one RPC or a block of execution. Information, such as the begin and end time of the span, a description, and additional information annotated for each span. Spans can be deeply nested; each span has information about its parent span and can span across network boundaries

9.1.3 Span Receivers

Span receivers, a.k.a. collectors, collect the spans from Trace and write to a store. Examples of these are LocalFileSpanReceiver, StandardOutSpanReceiver, ZipkinSpanReceiver, TraceMetricSource (the span receiver in Phoenix).

9.1.4 Setup

The Hadoop metrics framework (`https://hadoop.apache.org/docs/r2.7.2/api/org/apache/hadoop/metrics2/package-summary.html#instrumentation`) provides a way to produce and consume metrics using MetricsSource and MetricsSink. Phoenix provides a custom sink that receives the spans and traces from the client and server onto a default table SYSTEM.TRACING_STATS.

To enable tracing, changes need to be made on both the client and server end.

9.1.4.1 Client Configuration

Place the `hadoop-metrics2-phoenix.properties` file at the `${HBASE_CONF_DIR}` location.

```
# metrics sink impl class that collects the traces
phoenix.sink.tracing.class=org.apache.phoenix.trace.PhoenixMetricsSink
# Tell the sink where to write the metrics phoenix.sink.tracing.writer-
class=org.apache.phoenix.trace.PhoenixTableMetricsWriter
# Only handles traces with a context of "tracing". This ensures
phoenix.sink.tracing.context=tracing

# Sample from all the sources every 10 seconds
*.period=10

# chooses one of the following.
# never - equal to disabling tracing.
# always - trace every request
# Add below configutation properties in hbase-site.xml
# probability - does a sampling of request.
phoenix.tracing.frequency=[never | always | probability]

# used when the tracing frequency is set to 'probability'.
phoenix.trace.probability.threshold = 0.05
```

Apart from specifying the configuration in a properties file, you can configure tracing at a connection level. For example:

```
Properties props = new Properties();
props.setProperty("phoenix.trace.frequency", "probability");
props.setProperty("phoenix.trace.probability.threshold", 0.5)
final Connection conn = DriverManager.getConnection("jdbc:phoenix:localho
st", props);
```

9.1.4.2   Server Configuration

Similar to the setup on the client, we need to update the `hadoop-metrics2-hbase.` `properties` file at `${HBASE_CONF_DIR}` on the server.

```
# metrics sink impl class that collects the traces
phoenix.sink.tracing.class=org.apache.phoenix.trace.PhoenixMetricsSink
# Only handle traces with a context of "tracing". This ensures
phoenix.sink.tracing.context=tracing
# ensure that we receive traces on the server
hbase.sink.tracing.class=org.apache.phoenix.trace.PhoenixMetricsSink
# Tell the sink where to write the metrics
hbase.sink.tracing.writer-class=org.apache.phoenix.trace.
PhoenixTableMetricsWriter
# Only handle traces with a context of "tracing"
hbase.sink.tracing.context=tracing
```

By default, all traces are written to SYSTEM.TRACING_STATS. If you wish to change this, update the `hbase-site.xml` file with the following addition:

```
<property>
    <name>phoenix.trace.statsTableName</name>
    <value>{custom_tracing_table}</value>
</property>
```

Based on the frequency set, the trace requests wrapped in a MetricsRecord are written to the table. To view the contents of the table, open up Sqlline.py and run the following command:

```
$ bin/sqlline.py
```

You can enable and disable tracing at each request level by executing the following queries

```
$ 0: jdbc:phoenix:> TRACE ON;
```

```
$ 0: jdbc:phoenix:> TRACE OFF;
```

Trace information can be collected with sampling rates (range from 0 to 1). Changing tracing frequency of the query can improve the visualization; for example setting trace on with a sampling value of 0.5.

We can compute the metrics at a request level in the code. Phoenix takes this a step further and provides a web UI to better view the traces.

Start the tracing server by issuing the command at PHOENIX_HOME directory

```
$ ./bin/traceserver.py start
```

The above commands start a Jetty server locally on port 8864. To change these configurations, update `hbase-site.xml` on the client

```
<property>
    <name>phoenix.traceserver.http.port"</name>
    <value>8864</value>
</property>
```

The web UI provides a quick view of trace distributions, counts, dependencies, and timelines.

Gotchas:

With the above setup, we capture traces of the Phoenix API through Hadoop metrics. To get deeper insight into tracing of HBase and HDFS, you need to configure the necessary span receivers in `hbase-site.xml` and `hdfs-site.xml`. To streamline the trace collection, we could write a custom span receiver that writes the traces and spans to the same Phoenix table.

9.2 Phoenix Bulk Loading

Phoenix bulk load is a MapReduce job that allows loading of CSV and JSON datasets into Phoenix tables. This tool internally generates the necessary HFiles for the data table, which provides a high throughput and efficient usage of the cluster, better than `bin/psql.py` which uses the HBase Put API. We can also specify the index table name.

9.2.1 Setup

```
$export HADOOP_CLASSPATH = $(hbase mapredcp):/path-to-hbase-conf

# to load CSV data
$ hadoop jar phoenix-<version>-HBase-<hbase-version>-client.jar org.apache.
phoenix.mapreduce.CsvBulkLoadTool --table ORDERS --input orders.csv

# to load JSON data
$ hadoop jar phoenix-<version>-HBase-<hbase-version>-client.jar org.apache.
phoenix.mapreduce.JsonBulkLoadTool --table ORDERS --input orders.csv
```

Additional arguments

Table 9-1. Bulk Loading arguments

--input	Input path to data. Mandatory
--zookeeper	Zookeeper quorum uri
--schema	Schema of the data table.
--table	Data table. Mandatory
--index-table	Index table when we wish to load data to index table rather than
--import-columns	Comma separated list of columns
--ignore-errors	Ignore any errors that arise in the job.
--output	Output path where the intermediate HFiles are placed.
--delimiter	Delimiter to be used for CSV data only. Default is ','
--quote	Phrase delimiter used for CSV data only. Defaults to double quote
--array-delimiter	Delimiter for array elements. Defaults to ':'

9.2.2   Gotchas

1. The above job produces HFiles at the --output location specified. To ensure the subsequent step that loads the HFiles into HBase tables has the necessary permissions, we need to generate the files as user 'hbase'. Prefix the above commands with 'sudo -u hbase'.

2. When importing CSV data, if a column is of an array type, use a different delimiter to explicitly differentiate the array values. The default delimiter is ':'.

3. If the target table is a newly created Phoenix table, ensure the table is pre-split, as the number of reducers that run for the job depends on the number of regions for the table. By default, since there is only one region, you will notice degraded MapReduce performance as mutations end up on one reducer.

4. By default, bulk loading of HFiles with more than 32 per column family fails with an IOException. Either we can increase the region size from its default of 10 GB to a much larger number, or we can update the property '**hbase. mapreduce.bulkload.max.hfiles.perRegion.perFamily**' in hbase-site.xml

5. Bulk loading JSON data using the JsonBulkLoadTool job doesn't allow nested JSON structures. Also, lists in JSON are internally mapped as Array types in Phoenix.

9.3   Index Load Async

In the previous chapters, we have created both mutable and immutable indexes, and have observed that index population on an existing data table takes a long time due to its synchronous nature. Starting with Phoenix version 4.5, we can run index creation using an asynchronous approach by running a MapReduce job.

Let's see how to create an index table asynchronously through the following command.

```
CREATE INDEX index_name ON schema_name.table_name (columns) ASYNC
```

After running the command, Phoenix internally marks the index state as INACTIVE. After running the MapReduce job successfully, the index is ACTIVE and is served for querying.

```
$export HADOOP_CLASSPATH = $(hbase mapredcp):/path-to-hbase-conf
```

```
$ hadoop jar phoenix-<version>-HBase-<hbase-version>-client.jar org.apache.
phoenix.mapreduce.index.IndexTool
   --schema MY_SCHEMA --data-table MY_TABLE --index-table ASYNC_IDX
   --output-path /hdfs/path/for/hfiles
```

9.4   Pherf

Pherf is a tool, similar to Jmeter, which is part of the standard distribution that allows developers to configure scenarios of various queries which can be run on a standalone or a distributed cluster. The tool provides the ability to benchmark a cluster and helps the developer understand the impact of various configuration changes and new features on the cluster.

The Pherf tool records the times of both read and write operations, and can be configured to run with multiple threads with various test scenarios.

Each configured test requires a schema and a scenario. The schema file defines the schemas of the table and the respective indexes (if needed) that need to be created as a precursor to the performance test. Configuration is accomplished primarily using the Data Definition language.

The scenario file is an XML file where we define the data model of the columns and the rules that govern the data creation. Each scenario is a definition of the kind of data to be generated against the table, the number of rows to be upserted and the set of queries to be fired against the cluster.

In addition, for each column, based on the type, you can define rules like the length of the data, the data sequence (which can be either SEQUENTIAL or RANDOM), min and max values for numeric data type columns, fixed sets of values for dates along with the probability distribution of the number of rows containing them, and prefixes that can be used for string columns. Defining custom data generation rules helps modeling in data upsert and validation resembling the dataset of your needs.

Example **porders-schema.sql** file

```
# ORDER table DDL

CREATE TABLE IF NOT EXISTS PORDERS(
        ORDER_ID INTEGER NOT NULL,
        CUST_ID INTEGER NOT NULL,
         ORDER_DATE DATE,
         AMOUNT DECIMAL,
        QUANTITY INTEGER
CONSTRAINT PK PRIMARY KEY (ORDER_ID,CUST_ID)
)
```

Example porders-scenario.xml

```
<?xml version="1.0" encoding="UTF-8" standalone="yes"?>
<datamodel name="orders">
   <datamapping>
      <column>
         <!-- This column type defines what will generally happen
              to VARCHAR fields unless they are explicitly defined or
              overridden elsewhere -->
         <name>GENERAL_VARCHAR</name>
         <type>VARCHAR</type>
         <dataSequence>RANDOM</dataSequence>
         <length>10</length>
      </column>
      <column>
         <name>GENERAL_CHAR</name>
         <type>CHAR</type>
         <dataSequence>SEQUENTIAL</dataSequence>
         <length>15</length>
      </column>
      <column>
         <type>DATE</type>
         <!--SEQUENTIAL is unsupported for DATE -->
         <dataSequence>RANDOM</dataSequence>
         <!-- Number [0-100] that represents the probability of creating a
              null value -->
         <!-- The higher the number, the more like the value will returned
              will be null -->
         <!-- Leaving this tag out is equivalent to having a 0
              probability. i.e. never null -->
         <nullChance>0</nullChance>
         <minValue>1975</minValue>
         <maxValue>2025</maxValue>
         <name>GENERAL_DATE</name>
      </column>
```

```
<column>
    <type>DATE</type>
    <!--SEQUENTIAL is unsupported for DATE -->
    <dataSequence>RANDOM</dataSequence>
    <!-- Number [0-100] that represents the probability of creating a
        null value -->
    <!-- The higher the number, the more like the value will returned
        will be null -->
    <!-- Leaving this tag out is equivalent to having a 0 probability.
        i.e. never null -->
    <nullChance>0</nullChance>
    <useCurrentDate>true</useCurrentDate>
    <name>NOW_DATE</name>
</column>
<column>
    <type>DECIMAL</type>
    <dataSequence>RANDOM</dataSequence>
    <minValue>0</minValue>
    <maxValue>1</maxValue>

    <!-- Precision is limited to 18 -->
    <precision>18</precision>
    <!-- Number [0-100] that represents the probability of creating a
        null value -->
    <!-- The higher the number, the more like the value will returned
        will be null -->
    <!-- Leaving this tag out is equivalent to having a 0 probability.
        i.e. never null -->
    <nullChance>10</nullChance>
    <name>GENERAL_DECIMAL</name>
</column>
<column>
    <name>GENERAL_INTEGER</name>
    <type>INTEGER</type>
    <dataSequence>RANDOM</dataSequence>
    <minValue>1</minValue>
    <maxValue>999999</maxValue>
    <!-- Number [0-100] that represents the probability of creating a
        null value -->
    <!-- The higher the number, the more like the value will returned
        will be null -->
    <!-- Leaving this tag out is equivalent to having a 0 probability.
        i.e. never null -->
    <nullChance>0</nullChance>
</column>
<column>
    <type>DATE</type>
    <name>CREATED_DATE</name>
```

131

```
            <minValue>2000</minValue>
            <maxValue>2015</maxValue>
            <valuelist>
                <!-- Distributes randomly with equal chance of being picked -->
                <datavalue distribution="80">
                    <!-- Joda time format: yyyy-MM-dd HH:mm:ss.SSS ZZZ -->
                    <minValue>2016-09-15 00:01:00.000</minValue>
                    <maxValue>2016-09-15 11:00:00.000</maxValue>
                </datavalue>
                <datavalue distribution="10">
                    <value>2016-11-04 00:01:00.000</value>
                </datavalue>
                <datavalue distribution="10">
                    <minValue>2016-12-25 00:01:00.000</minValue>
                    <maxValue>2016-12-31 00:01:00.300</maxValue>
                </datavalue>
            </valuelist>
        </column>
        <column>
            <type>CHAR</type>
            <userDefined>true</userDefined>
            <dataSequence>LIST</dataSequence>
            <length>15</length>
            <name>PARENT_ID</name>
            <valuelist>
                <!-- Distributes according to specified values. These must
                    total 100 -->
                <datavalue distribution="60">
                    <value>aAAyYhnNbBs9kWk</value>
                </datavalue>
                <datavalue distribution="20">
                    <value>bBByYhnNbBs9kWu</value>
                </datavalue>
                <datavalue distribution="20">
                    <value>cCCyYhnNbBs9kWr</value>
                </datavalue>
            </valuelist>
        </column>
        <column>
            <name>PREFX_STRING</name>
            <type>VARCHAR</type>
            <length>10</length>
            <userDefined>true</userDefined>
            <dataSequence>RANDOM</dataSequence>
            <prefix>MYPRFX</prefix>
        </column>
    </datamapping>
```

```
<scenarios>
    <scenario tableName="PORDERS" rowCount="1000" name="perf_read_writes">

        <!--
            This is used to add mixed R/W workloads.

            If this tag exists, a writer pool will be created based on
                the below properties.
            These props will override the default values in pherf.
                properties, but only for this
            scenario.The write jobs will run in conjunction with the
                querySet below.
        -->
        <writeParams executionDurationInMs="10000">
            <writerThreadCount>10</writerThreadCount>

            <!--
                Throttles the writers with a small sleep durations between
                writes.
            -->
            <threadSleepDuration>10</threadSleepDuration>
            <batchSize>1000</batchSize>
        </writeParams>
        <querySet concurrency="1" executionType="PARALLEL"
            executionDurationInMs="10000">
            <query id="q1" statement="select count(*) from PORDERS"/>
            <query id="q2" statement="select sum(QUANTITY) from PORDERS"/>
        </querySet>

    </scenario>
    </scenarios>
</datamodel>
```

9.4.1   Setup to Run the Test

The Phoenix distribution comes with both pherf-standalone.py and pherf-cluster.py.

1. Copy the **porders-schema.sql** to the directory ${PHOENIX_
    HOME}/bin/config/datamodel/

2. Copy the **porders-scenario.xml** to the directory

    ```
    ${PHOENIX_HOME}/bin/config/scenario/
    ```

3. Run the tool

```
$ ./bin/pherf-standalone.py -z localhost:2181 -scenarioFile .*porders-
scenario.xml -schemaFile .*porders-schema.sql -d -export -l
```

Arguments

Table 9-2. *pherf attributes*

Key	Description
-l	Apply the schema and load data.
-q	Executes the queries
-z	Zookeeper quorum
-scenarioFile	Path to the scenario file
-schemaFile	Path to the schema file
-export	Exports the results to CSV.
-diff	Compares the results of two runs
-drop	Drops and recreates the tables.
-stat	Update the SYSTEM.STATS table
-d	Debug mode
-listFiles	Command to display the schema and scenario files that the tool can read.

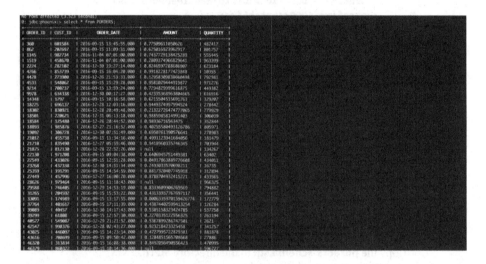

The results of the run are dumped onto the RESULTS directory in the folder from which you ran the above command.

9.4.2   Gotchas

Though Pherf is a great tool to do quick performance benchmarks, it doesn't do query result validation. It can execute queries but cannot validate if the results returned are correct.

9.5 Summary

In this chapter we discussed Phoenix performance configurations and how to tune them, tracing Phoenix for debugging purposes and knowing what is happening inside Phoenix. The Phoenix team is now trying to keep separate query parser to improve performance and integration with other frameworks. Separating parsing and other query processing activities will improve load balancing of phoenix and make this more component oriented pluggable architecture.

Index

A

ALTER tables
    columns, 56
    deleting/replacing columns, 56
    rename, 57
Apache Phoenix. *See* Phoenix

B

Big data source
    Apache Phoenix analytics, 14
    data warehouse
        and querying, 13
    Phoenix, 12
    RDBMSs, 13
    relational databases, 13
    traditional DBA problem, 12
Big data sources, 1–2
    analysis, 4
    applications (*see* Modern
        applications)
    Hadoop (*see* Hadoop ecosystem)
    lake and representation, 2
    transactional data, 2
Bulk loading, 127
    arguments, 128
    gotchas, 128
    setup, 127
Business Intelligence (BI), 5

C

Clauses
    GROUP BY, 58
    HAVING, 59
    LIMIT, 57
    ORDER BY, 59
    WHERE, 58
Clickstream logs, 3
Cloudera Hadoop, 30–31
Constraints, 51
Covered index, 99
CRUD
    data types, 37
        complex, 37–38
        primitive, 37
    SQL commands, 39–40
        ALTER, 42
        CREATE, 41
        DELETE, 42
        DESCRIBE, 42
        HELP, 40
        LIST, 43
        SELECT, 41
        UPSERT, 41

D

DROP TABLE command, 55

E

EQUIJOIN, 63

F

Flume integration
    configuration, 121
    run command, 122
    setup, 121
Functional indexes, 100

■ G

Global indexes, 92
Gotchas, 109
Group joins, 67

■ H

Hadoop Distributed File
        System (HDFS), 6, 123
    components and data storage, 6
    DataNodes, 6
    NameNode, 6
    secondary NameNode, 6
Hadoop ecosystem, 5
    HBase, 9–10
    HDFS, 6
    Hive, 10–11
    integration, 111
    MapReduce (*see* MapReduce)
    Oozie, 11
    overview, 5
    Phoenix, 12
    role of Phoenix, 32
        comparison, 33
        HBase, 32
    stack, 5
    ZooKeeper, 11
HBase, 9–10
HBase installation, 18
Hive, 10–11
    integration, 118
    setup, 118
    table creation, 119
Hortonworks Hadoop distribution
        platform (HDP), 20
    HBase, 27
    Phoenix shell, 29
    sandbox distribution, 21
        core jars verification, 26
        Hadoop password creation, 23
        HBase property modification, 27
        installation, 23
        Phoenix download, 24–25
        prerequisites, 25
        VirtualBox, 21–22
        VM, 22
    testing, 28, 30

■ I

Immutable tables, 94–95
    consistency, 95
    mutable tables, 96
        configuration, 96
        consistency, 96
Index load async, 129
Inner join, 63
Integration, 111
    Dataframe, 117
    Flume, 121
    Hadoop ecosystem, 111
    Hive, 118
    MapReduce, 111
    Pig, 120
    Spark, 115

■ J, K

Join query, 63
    group joins, 67
    inner join, 63
    optimizations, 69
        algorithm, 70
        configuration
            properties, 70
        types and cache storage, 71
    outer join
        FULL OUTER JOIN, 66–67
        LEFT OUTER JOIN, 64–65
        RIGHT OUTER JOIN, 65–66
    subqueries
        (*see* Subqueries)

■ L

Linux, 17
Local index, 96
    components, 97
    intractions, 97–98
    syntax, 98
Logical operators
    AND, 60
    BETWEEN, 61
    IN, 60
    LIKE, 61
    OR, 60

■ M

Mac OS X, 18
MapReduce
    integration, 111
    Map tasks, 7
    processing data, 9
    reduce phase, 8
    reduce stage, 7
    shuffle and reduce tasks, 7
    word count processing, 7
Modern applications, 3
    banking sector, 3
    fraud detection, 3
    log data analysis, 3
    recommendation engines, 4
    social Media, 4
Multiversion concurrency control, 85
Multi-versioned concurrency
        control (MVCC), 85

■ N

NOT NULL constraint, 51

■ O

Oozie, 11
Optimistic concurrency control, 85
Outer join
    FULL OUTER JOIN, 66–67
    LEFT OUTER JOIN, 64–65
    RIGHT OUTER JOIN, 65–66

■ P, Q

Paged queries, 75
    LIMIT and OFFSET, 76
    Row Value Constructor (RVC), 76
Pherf, 129–133
    attributes, 134
    gotchas, 134
    setup, 133
Phoenix, 15
    architecture, 16
    capabilities, 31–32
    Cloudera Hadoop, 30–31
    Hadoop ecosystem
        (see Hadoop ecosystem)

HBase, 18
history of, 15
Hortonworks HDP (see Hortonworks
        Hadoop distribution platform)
installation, 17
    binary distribution, 19
    HBase, 20
    local HBase, 20
Java installation, 17
    Linux, 17
    Mac OS X, 18
multi-tenancy, 34
query server, 35
secondary indexes, 34
skip scan, 34
SQL driver (HBase), 15–16
transactions, 33, 86
    committing transactions, 89
    hbase-site.xml, 87
    limitations, 90
    properties, 86
    tables, 89
    Tephra configuration, 87
user-defined functions, 33
view syntax, 34
Phoenix Query Server (PQS)
    client, 107
    configuration properties, 108
    directories and
        start server, 107
    download, 107
    features, 109
    Gotchas, 109
    installation, 107
    interaction, 106
    setup, 107
    usage, 108
Pig
    integration, 120
        data access, 120
        PhoenixHBaseStorage, 120
        setup, 120

■ R

Relational database management
        system (RDBMS), 13
ROLLBACK, 80
Row Value Constructor (RVC), 75, 76

■ S

Salted tables, 53
SAVEPOINT, 81
Secondary indexes, 91
    covered index, 99
    data tables/views, 91
    functional indexes, 100
    global indexes, 92
    immutable tables
        (*see* Immutable tables)
    local index, 96
        components, 97
        intractions, 97–98
        syntax, 98
SET TRANSACTION, 81
Spark integration, 115
SQL transactions, 79
Subjoins. Group joins
Subqueries
    ANY, SOME and ALL, 73
    EXISTS and NOT EXISTS clauses, 72
    IN and NOT IN, 72
    nested query, 71
    UPSERT statements, 73

■ T

Table creation, 52
Tephra, 85
Tracing server, 123
    client configuration, 124
    multiple spans, 124
    server configuration, 125–127
    setup, 124
    span receivers, 124
    trace, 123
Transactions
    COMMIT, 80
    HBase, 81
        commit, 83
        components, 82
        integration, 81–82

    lifecycle, 84
    multiversion concurrency
        control, 85
    optimistic concurrency control, 85
    processor coprocessor, 83
    TransactionAware client, 82
    transaction manager, 82
HBaserowkey, 81
Phoenix
    committing transactions, 89
    hbase-site.xml, 87
    limitations, 90
    properties, 86
    tables, 89
    Tephra configuration, 87
properties
    atomicity, 80
    consistency, 80
    durability, 80
    isolation, 80
ROLLBACK, 80
SAVEPOINT, 81
SET TRANSACTION, 81
SQL transactions, 79
Tephra, 85

■ U

UPSERT statements, 73
User defined functions (UDF), 91, 102
    advantages, 102
    configuration properties, 105
    custom creation, 102–104
    runtime environment, 105–106

■ V, W, X, Y

Views, 74

■ Z

ZooKeeper, 11

Get the eBook for only $4.99!

Why limit yourself?

Now you can take the weightless companion with you wherever you go and access your content on your PC, phone, tablet, or reader.

Since you've purchased this print book, we are happy to offer you the eBook for just $4.99.

Convenient and fully searchable, the PDF version enables you to easily find and copy code—or perform examples by quickly toggling between instructions and applications.

To learn more, go to http://www.apress.com/us/shop/companion or contact support@apress.com.

Printed in the United States
By Bookmasters